high vibration

how to
get back to
work

steve wharton

foulsham
LONDON • NEW YORK • TORONTO • SYDNEY

foulsham

The Publishing House, Bennetts Close, Cippenham, Slough, Berkshire, SL1 5AP, England

ISBN 0-572-03078-9

Copyright © 2005 Steven Hamilton

Cover photograph by Powerstock

A CIP record for this book is available from the British Library

The moral right of the author has been asserted

Printed in Great Britain by Cox & Wyman Ltd, Reading, Berkshire

Contents

Dedicated to the memory of Joe, my father.

I love you.

Getting Back to Work

Being out of work for a while can happen to anybody. It may be that you have taken time out to raise a family or to do some travelling; it may be that you have been ill; or it may be that you have been made redundant or have had a gap between jobs. Many of us have experienced a break in our employment at some time.

Even those who are lucky enough not to have been out of work know how hard it is to motivate yourself to get back into the work routine after a holiday. If you are returning to work after a longer gap, it is much more difficult. When you are out of work for any length of time, you develop new routines and start to see things from a different perspective. These ways of doing and looking at things can be very different from those you need when you are in a regular job.

Your employment potential is hugely influenced by your thought processes. High-vibrational thinking (or HVT) will give you an insight into exactly what is taking place within your mind, helping you to break it down to the nuts and bolts so that you have more control over the way you think. It will show you how you form new opinions and how these can become rigid thought patterns, rooted deep within your mind. It will help you to look at your expectations of yourself and see how influential they are in determining the path your life will take, and it will empower you in ways that will make your life easier, giving you control over all the negatives that used to control you. With your new and confident approach, you will be able to make the best of your capabilities, and the transition back to work will be a much smoother and more comfortable process.

One of the biggest hurdles to overcome in returning to work is learning how to motivate yourself. This book will explain why that is and also give you the tools to rekindle your drive and ambition. Indeed, HVT will give you more than that, as you begin to realise just what you are capable of and learn to believe in yourself. You will start to push the boundaries of your self-imposed limitations and reach for your true potential.

HVT will benefit you in many areas of your life, as the basic principles can be adapted to any subject. Shining the powerful light of HVT on the problems associated with getting back to work will give you an indication of the tremendous potential of this approach, and your new-found sense of control will empower you to step into a new and positive future.

Our World of Energy

'If you want to find the secrets of the universe, think in terms of energy, frequency and vibration.' Dr Nikola Tesla, 1942

Dr Nikola Tesla was one of the foremost scientists of the early twentieth century. His outstanding intellect paved the way for a large number of modern technological developments; in fact the tesla coil is still used in many television sets today. It is amazing to think that his words in 1942 should be still so relevant today. We now know that his understanding of the universe as energy, frequency and vibration was quite accurate. As we explore the intricate workings of the universe, unlocking the secrets of this amazing world of energy in which we live, this fact only becomes clearer.

Nothing you see around you is quite as it seems! The world that we live in is a huge ocean of energy, taking many different forms. The age of the microscope has shown us abundantly clearly that things that appear solid and static to us are in fact nothing of the sort. Even if the only science you know has been learnt from TV dramas about forensic scientists, you will be aware that if you look at an apparently solid object at a sufficiently powerful magnification, you will find that it is made up not of a single solid substance but of tiny particles vibrating at phenomenal speed. These tiny particles are known as neutrons, electrons and protons, and they link together to form atoms, the most basic building blocks of life.

What is perhaps even more astonishing is that atoms actually consist of 90 per cent empty space, which – by logical deduction – means that what we think of as solid, such as a concrete wall, is in fact mostly not solid at all! Nothing around us is actually solid, even though it may appear so; everything is made up of energy, vibrating constantly and at various frequencies. This applies to everything you see around you: trees, houses, cars, walls, roads, dogs, cats, fish. It is a fundamental law of physics and applies even to us humans.

Each of these millions upon millions of different forms of energy vibrates at a specific frequency. The frequency at which it vibrates influences the form of the object. For example, the molecules of a solid vibrate very slowly; the molecules of a liquid vibrate more quickly; and the molecules of a gas vibrate even more quickly. Thus something with the same chemical composition can take different forms depending on the vibrational frequency of its molecules. When the molecules are vibrating at a medium frequency rate, water appears as a liquid. Slow down that frequency and you get ice; speed up the frequency and you get steam.

We are all part of the vibrant ocean of energy

As I have said, we are just as much a part of this cycle of energy as everything else around us. High-vibrational thinking is based on that fact. Its fundamental principal is that we need to learn to see and think about our world in terms of energy.

High-vibrational thinking is a revolutionary new concept that teaches us how to have some control over the incredible universe of energy that we live in. It offers a way of seeing people – and the interactions between people – as part of a unique energy transmission process that is hugely empowering to the individual. The first part of this book explains exactly how the system works. If you go back to fundamentals, it is really very easy to understand.

Just as ice, water and steam vibrate at different frequencies, so emotional energy also vibrates at different frequencies. As I will be explaining in detail later, positive emotions are high-vibrational energies, while negative emotions are low-vibrational energies. If we can find a way to maintain high-vibrational energy and deflect low-vibrational energy, then we can change our whole perspective on life. That's what HVT can help us to do. HVT is a system that takes positive thinking into an exciting new dimension.

HVT changes your perspective

This realisation throws a whole new light on how we perceive our world. Indeed, knowing how to use this information – and I'll be showing you that too – can be hugely liberating and empowering, because it offers a way of using our knowledge to handle our lives in a more beneficial and productive way. This new perspective gives you far greater control over everyday situations and events that you may previously have thought were largely beyond your control. With this knowledge comes power, and that power is the ability to choose more carefully how you relate to the energies that affect your life.

HVT will become automatic

What's more, once you have learnt how to use this power, it will become an automatic way of thinking, and you can gain the benefits without even having to make a conscious choice about it. Once you have learnt to walk, you don't need to think consciously about the process any more. It's the same with HVT. Once you understand HVT, you will find that you automatically begin to incorporate it into your life as a working practice without any conscious effort on your part. Its positive influence on your life will be automatic, as the truth of HVT, once learnt, cannot be ignored. Using HVT on a daily basis becomes a natural habit that will benefit every aspect of your life and help you to change in a positive and fulfilling way. All of a sudden, you will find that something inside you is monitoring the events and situations in your life and automatically responding to negative situations in a way that will prevent them from dragging down the frequency of your energy field and making you feel bad.

A paradigm shift in consciousness occurs when you use HVT. You find yourself able to deal with the negative events and situations that are part of everyday life in a new and positive way. HVT enables you to take control of events and situations rather than allowing them to control you. This is incredibly liberating, freeing your mind to direct your life in a much more productive and focused way.

Let's look at a simple example from an HVT course I recently ran. Within days of attending the course, two of my students found themselves turning off a particular television programme that they had been watching regularly for many years. They did not think about this action consciously until weeks later when it came up in conversation. Another student was talking about how negative this television programme had become. At that point, they both realised they had made the decision not to watch it any more immediately after attending the HVT course. Subconsciously they had sensed its negative impact and put a stop to it.

This kind of reaction is common among people who attend HVT courses, because they quickly learn to avoid engaging with damaging negative energies. You are already starting to learn that lesson simply by reading this book.

You too can learn automatically to handle situations and decisions in a more positive and beneficial way.

Essentially simple

The real strength of HVT is its simplicity and the fact that when applied to any subject it breaks it down to a few basics. This enables anybody, whatever their age or background, to gain an understanding that previously may have seemed impossible. This is one of the reasons we have had so much success in working with children as young as ten years old. Young people absorb the concept very quickly and find it easy to think in terms of HVT about every area of their life.

It also means that the technique can be applied to any aspect of your life, regardless of your occupation or lifestyle. At school, it can give your more confidence and enthusiasm and help you to perform well. At work, it can cut out negativity, create a better atmosphere and even increase productivity. In the home, it can reduce arguments and create a more loving environment.

Essentially, HVT is about making you feel good about yourself and maintaining that feel-good factor whatever life throws at you. Just think how much happier that could make you – not to mention the immeasurable stride forwards in terms of moving our world into a brighter, high-vibrational future.

How Emotional Energy Vibrates

Now we understand that the whole world is part of a complex energy system, let's look specifically at how that affects us. Here, we are talking in terms of the power of emotional energy, and that is what we can harness to work to our advantage with HVT.

We have seen that – just like the objects around us – we are made up of energy and – like all forms of energy – our personal energy field vibrates constantly. The vibrational frequency of our energy field is affected by our thoughts and feelings. These are also made up of energy waves, and they influence our lives much more profoundly than we may realise. So depending on how we are feeling at any given time, the frequency at which our energy field vibrates can change dramatically.

Scientists and researchers in the USA have measured the frequency of the energy waves transmitted by the emotion of love, which they found vibrate very quickly, or at a very high frequency. Similarly, they measured the frequency of the energy waves transmitted by the emotion of fear, which they found vibrate very slowly, or at a low frequency. Our world exists within these two parameters.

Love is transmitted on a short wavelength, so it has a fast, high-vibrational frequency.

Fear is transmitted on a long wavelength, so it has a slow, low-vibrational frequency.

Think for a moment about listening to the radio, and this will help you to understand how energy waves work. Radio stations are constantly transmitting radio waves. These are in the air all around us, even though we cannot actually see them. If your radio is not tuned in to the right frequency, all you will hear is an annoying hiss. However, if you tune in your radio to the right frequency, you will be able to pick up on those radio waves so that you can hear and understand them perfectly, whether they are transmitting music, news, drama or comedy.

Happy is a high vibration
So whatever we are thinking and feeling has a very real effect, as it alters the frequency of our personal energy field. If we are happy, our energy is high-vibrational; if we are sad, our energy is low-vibrational. I am sure you are already getting the idea. Similarly, we can be affected by other people's thoughts and feelings. If you are unlucky enough to be in a room full of bored or unhappy people, it is very hard to remain upbeat and cheerful.

When we are full of laughter and joy, it makes us feel good. What is actually happening is that the high-vibrational energy of joy has pushed up the frequency of our personal energy field. We also experience this effect when we achieve something good, such as passing a driving test or an exam, scoring a goal, winning a competition, or receiving praise for a job well done. What is happening here is the same: the achievement has made us feel suddenly successful and good about ourselves, again pushing up the frequency of our personal energy field.

So, as you can see, any thoughts and feelings that are positive – laughter, joy, honesty, sincerity, truth, compassion – are high-vibrational, keeping our energy field vibrating at the higher levels and therefore making us feel good. Just think about some of the expressions we use to describe that kind of feeling: 'I'm high as a kite', 'I'm buzzing', 'My mind's racing'. They are referring to the frequency of our personal energy field, and they clearly demonstrate that wonderful elation. The faster our energy field vibrates, the better we feel, because that means we are closer to the frequency of love.

Of course, the opposite is also true. Anger, frustration, hate, jealousy, envy, greed and selfishness are all negative thoughts and feelings. Such emotions are low-vibrational; they slow down our energy field and make us feel bad. This is why we use phrases such as 'I'm down in the dumps' or 'I'm flat as a pancake'. The lower our energy field vibrates, the closer we are to the vibration of fear – which is not where we want to be!

Increasing our vibrational frequency

Even though this may be the first time you have thought about it in these terms, you will probably recognise that we spend most of our time trying to feel good about ourselves. In HVT terms, that means we are constantly seeking to increase our vibrational energy frequency.

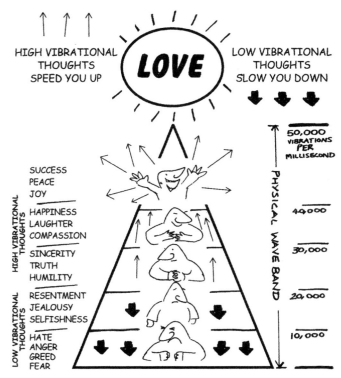

Hypothetically speaking, the physical waveband may run from 0 to 50,000 vibrations per millisecond. Our energy fields fluctuate between these parameters in our day-to-day lives. When we are happy and enjoying life, we may be vibrating at 35,000 vibrations per millisecond, but this may fall to 6,000 vibrations per millisecond when we are down in the dumps.

There are any number of ways to try to do this – getting your hair done, buying new clothes, having a drink, going to the gym, planning a special night out. They can all be effective, but if they don't alter your fundamental emotional state, the effect is not going to last very long. If you have ever got a buzz from buying a new pair of shoes, only to feel low again by the time you got home because you had nowhere to go to show them off, you'll know what I mean.

Some people take the search for a high to extremes, experimenting with drink and drugs. This may give a temporary 'high' but can very soon have the serious negative result of addiction.

That's where HVT comes in, because it is a way of educating ourselves so that our normal vibrational frequency is higher – plus it teaches us to control the effects of low-vibrational energy from other sources. It's just like exercising regularly to increase your resting heart rate. This not only makes you feel fitter but it also makes it easier for you to cope with the physical demands of your everyday life.

How Our Emotional Frequency Is Established

As we spend most of our time trying to raise our vibrational frequency in order to feel better about ourselves, it makes sense to have a look at the factors that determine our individual energy level in the first place. This is established and controlled primarily by our subconscious mind.

The conscious and subconscious mind

Your conscious mind is what you use to go about your everyday life – paying the bills, cleaning, sorting the washing, going to work. This is the methodical, reasoning part of your mind that carries out the daily tasks. It is the organised, sensible, logical part of you that understands how your world works. Your conscious mind automatically analyses any situation it confronts and plots the best and most logical way to deal with it.

Your subconscious mind, on the other hand, is a more complex entity, and is a source of immense power. It is affected by your surroundings in much more subtle ways and reacts most strongly to emotional stimuli.

Many psychologists refer to the subconscious mind as the 'inner child', because they feel that this best describes its characteristics. This terminology can help us to understand why our subconscious can sometimes pull us towards something that is not good for us. Imagine yourself as a child of five years old, with all the feelings and wonderment you had at that age; now imagine that this child is real and living inside you. Now you have a picture of your subconscious mind. It does not reflect you as you are now, with everything you have experienced and learnt over the course of a lifetime, but you as you were then. This child has no concept of what is good or bad for

Your inner child (your subconscious mind) will do everything it can to keep you in your comfort zone, even if this means holding you back in your life.

you; it just has its programming, which it will try to stick to regardless of what you may or may not consciously want.

In other words, we are all going through life trying to make some kind of progress but subject to the limitations that our subconscious mind places upon us. In terms of energy, our subconscious monitors us on a daily basis to keep us in what it has defined as our normal vibrational frequency zone.

Our formative years

The most important factor in determining this normal or average vibrational frequency level is the first five or six years of our lives. It is during these formative years that we establish our general thought patterns about ourselves. These first five or six years effectively programme our subconscious mind with certain beliefs about ourselves, which we then carry throughout the rest of our lives and which are very difficult to change. This vibrational frequency programming sets the boundaries for us and has a major bearing on every aspect of our life from then on.

The most influential factors in our development are our immediate family and the environment we grow up in. In other words, the vibrational frequency of our environment and the frequency level of our family are what we pick up and become used to as our norm. When our mind is young and impressionable during those early years, we readily accept the situation in which we find ourselves. Because we don't know of any other situation, we unquestioningly believe that this is where we belong. This becomes the frequency zone we feel comfortable in and which, subconsciously, we spend virtually the rest of our lives trying to stay in.

So if you were brought up in a family with not much love (high-vibrational energy), you will believe that you only deserve a certain amount of love in your life, and your subconscious will use all its power to make sure that that is what happens. This will have massive repercussions, affecting your relationships, your work – in fact, everything you do in life. Your subconscious will stick to the programming, whether it's good for you or bad for you. In other words, it will monitor your vibrational frequency and keep it at the level that it is programmed to do.

As we grow up, our subconscious beliefs tend to become self-confirming because we constantly play them over in our subconscious mind, reaffirming our opinions and thoughts about ourselves. Most of the time, we are completely unaware that we are doing this. When we are constantly affirming to ourselves that we are not worthy (worthy meaning deserving of love, the highest-vibrational energy), we are keeping our vibrational frequency at the lower levels – and making life much harder for ourselves. The opposite is also true. If we constantly circulate high-vibrational thoughts about ourselves, we will keep our vibrational frequency at the higher levels, which in turn affirms that we are worthy and makes our life run much more smoothly.

Your inner child (subconscious mind) is much more in control of your life than you realise.

Of course, we have to acknowledge that we are all different and unique individuals with many varying factors determining our personality. This is why different people emerge from a similar upbringing with a different attitude to life. However, you are almost certainly reading this book because at least one aspect of your life can be improved, and understanding where any negative input may have come from is the first step towards being able to change the negative and maximise the positive.

The comfort zone

The energy level that we feel is where we belong is often referred to as our 'comfort zone'. We find it very difficult to break out of this zone, as our subconscious mind constantly draws us back to it as its starting point, regardless of whether it is in fact good for us or bad for us. This may seem strange but is in fact quite logical.

We tend to mix and feel more comfortable with people of a similar vibration rate.

You may, for example, feel uncomfortable in an upmarket, expensive restaurant, or perhaps you feel nervous when talking to professional people such as lawyers or consultants. What you are experiencing is a reaction to the frequency of the environment or person – if the frequency is vibrating at a higher rate than yours, you will probably feel slightly uncomfortable. This means you will seek out places and people with which you share a similar frequency, as this is where you naturally feel most comfortable.

Imagine carrying around with you an identity card that has not only all your personal details but also all your unconscious beliefs about yourself printed on it. If your normal vibrational frequency is low, your ID might list some of the following:

▶ You will only be shown a limited amount of affection from people who are close to you
▶ You are only allowed to have a low-paid job
▶ You are only allowed to live in a small house
▶ You are only allowed to have an old car
▶ You are only allowed to be average in what you do
▶ You are only allowed to wear casual clothes
▶ You will only be able to achieve a limited amount of success
▶ You will only ever have difficult relationships
▶ You will only ever have friends who take advantage of you

Now imagine that if you try to step out of line by going against these guidelines, you will be confronted by a police officer whose job it is to keep you within their confines. Let's say you manage to get a good job that pays well. Before you know it, the officer is on your case and starts talking you out of the job. You may find that you can't motivate yourself to raise your level of achievement as you need to in order to do the job well, so you start to make excuses and lay the blame elsewhere. Instead, you tell yourself that you work too hard or the firm is taking advantage of you, the pay is not adequate or you are not appreciated. This undermines your confidence and your ability to do the job well, and before very long you will find a way to give up the job while blaming everyone else.

I have seen this happen in my own experience. A very capable employee suddenly, after about three months in the job, begins to under perform. They start coming in late with any old feeble excuse, they cultivate an attitude of not been appreciated, they disrupt the other staff and in the end they push you so far that you have no choice but to let them go. When this happens, they insist that they are being victimised, they have done nothing wrong, and they may even threaten to take you to a tribunal. What they fail to acknowledge – even to themselves – is that it is their own behaviour that has caused the problem. The police officer has done his job and dragged them back into their low-vibrational comfort zone.

The problem with this situation is that we don't realise what is happening – that it is our own subconscious mind that is wreaking such havoc in our lives. It does not seem logical to believe that we would sabotage our own efforts, so we assume that the fault lies elsewhere.

I have experienced this myself, so I know how easily it can occur. When I was at school I was quite good at sport and soon found myself playing for the school teams. I did very well, and at one point it was expected that I might go on to a higher level. Once I realised that this was in prospect, I couldn't seem to motivate myself any more and decided to stop playing altogether. At the time, I just decided that I didn't feel like playing any more; it was only years later that I realised what had taken place. The threat of success had triggered off my subconscious programming, which dictated that I didn't deserve the high-frequency feelings that success could bring. These would have pushed me out of my comfort zone and into a new higher-frequency zone, so my subconscious mind convinced me that I didn't like sports any more and made me feel tired and unmotivated when faced with a game. Unfortunately for me, my subconscious won, and at 14 years of age I hung up my boots and as a result missed many years of enjoyment.

Not better but different
One thing always to remember, however, is that even if you start out with a low-vibrational energy field and feel uncomfortable with a different group of people, they are not 'better' than you. We all have our own qualities, strengths and weaknesses. You may want to be more like someone who has a high-vibrational energy field because they are fun to be around and are positive and more successful – that's fine. But that doesn't make them intrinsically better than you. Envy and self-criticism are both low-vibrational emotions, and if you give way to them, it will only make things worse.

You may, on the other hand, be someone who has had a good upbringing in a high-vibrational environment, leaving you with high-vibrational thought patterns. This gives you a much better chance of making the most of your life and better equips you to take advantage of opportunities that arise. You will still feel uncomfortable in places or with people where the energy pattern does not match your own – probably because your personal energy field is vibrating at a higher frequency – but it is important that you do not fall into the trap of believing that this makes you better in some way, for this is a damaging thought pattern. Arrogance and self-importance will pull down your energy frequency.

Don't try to place blame

It is important to point out here that your parents and their parents before them were also subject to this subconscious programming. However they brought you up, they were doing their best within their own programmed mental confines.

It is essential that you do not try to attach blame to anybody for your life as it stands at the moment. This would be to go straight down the low-vibrational route. Such thought processes are negative and low-frequency; they are certain to act as a dead weight around your neck and pull you down. Pointing the finger at others serves no purpose and will only harm you – by lowering your vibrational frequency. This is the time to assess the past and move on to the new, high-vibrational you.

How Our Emotional Frequency Affects Our Lives

The easiest way to demonstrate how limiting it can be to allow your subconscious mind to remain in control of your life is to look at a few examples.

Paul's comfort zone with crime

A few years ago, my work brought me into contact with a sales representative who proceeded to tell me a bit about himself. Let's call him Paul. Paul was brought up in a fairly tough environment, and his father had not been around much, as he had spent most of his time in prison for relatively minor offences. However, this childhood grounding had taken its toll, and, at 12 years old, Paul had found himself in trouble with the police for the first time for a minor crime. His family considered crime as a profession and accepted it as a normal way of life so, far from chastising him for having committed a crime, they were more concerned that he had not got away with it. This pathway continued. Paul's teenage years were littered with offences, but since he was behaving exactly according to his own idea of normality, he could see nothing unacceptable in this.

At the age of 25, during another stay in prison, Paul decided to go straight. He left prison with good intentions, found himself a job and at first managed to stay on the straight and narrow. It wasn't long, however, before he found himself drawn back to crime, even though he tried not to be tempted. When I spoke to him, he was very disappointed with himself and said that no matter how hard he tried, he kept finding himself committing offences. Although this made him feel bad about himself, when the temptation was there, he just could not resist it.

I wish I could tell you that this story has a happy ending, but I lost contact with Paul many years ago and do not know how his life has turned out. However, over the years, I have given Paul's story a great deal of thought. When I began to understand the workings of the subconscious mind, it became clear to me exactly what his problem was. Even though Paul wanted to stop being drawn to crime, his subconscious mind (inner child) did not. To his subconscious mind, crime was defined as normal behaviour – because this is what it had been programmed with during his first five or six years – and so was safely in his comfort zone. When, as an adult, Paul wanted to break out of his comfort zone, his subconscious mind took every opportunity to draw him back in.

When you think about how deep-rooted and fundamental our subconscious mind is to our entire personality, it is hardly surprising that it is very influential. We all have to contend with the daily tussle with our subconscious mind, but when we understand that it is simply trying to keep us within the boundaries of our own comfort zone, we have taken the first step towards doing something to take control over it.

Sue's comfort zone with food
Another friend of mine – let's call her Sue – has spent the last year or so trying to lose weight – something many of us have struggled with at some time. She has tried every

kind of diet, with the same results: she loses a few pounds at the beginning, but a few weeks later the weight is back on. Then it's on to the next diet regime. She has fallen into the trap of yoyo dieting and is unable to maintain her ideal weight for any length of time. So why is it so difficult for Sue – like many of us – to get into new eating habits and stick to them?

Let's take a careful look at what is happening here. When Sue begins the diet, she really wants to lose weight and is fully motivated. She has the necessary willpower to control her eating habits. She knows that she will feel better and be healthier if she eats well and maintains the right weight for her height and build. The principles are easy enough to understand: eat the right amount of the right foods and she will lose weight. And with the range of healthy food options available these days, there is never even any need for her to feel hungry. Nevertheless, after the first few weeks, or even days, she finds herself drifting back into bad eating habits. Sue's favourite tactic is to move the goal posts. Having decided that she wanted to lose weight for an up-and-coming holiday, she then decides it's for her daughter's graduation ceremony, then for Christmas, then for the new year, and so on.

The problem is, of course, that Sue is obeying her inner child. Her subconscious is telling her that the unhealthy diet she has become used to or has cultivated over the years is what she should be eating. This kind of food is her comfort zone, and it is very difficult to leave it. 'No, you can't have any chocolate or sweets and you must eat plenty of fresh vegetables' isn't what Sue's inner child wants to hear. Sue's initial determination will control the child for a while, but very soon the child's persistence will be rewarded, because it just feels right to go back to your comfort zone.

Jim's comfort zone with keeping fit

Jim's story is another good example of how the subconscious mind sabotages our efforts to instigate change. When Jim first went to the gym he was filled with enthusiasm and energy for his get-fit project. Sure enough, the first few visits were easy, as he raced around the equipment, lifting weights, doing sit-ups and so on, quite possibly overdoing it in his eagerness to succeed. Then, after a while, the novelty wore off. Jim started to accept the feeblest excuses for not going to the gym – 'I have to take the dog for a walk', 'I feel a bit tired' and (an old favourite of many of us) 'I haven't got time'. Of course, just as Jim's initial determination had begun to wear off, his subconscious mind had kicked in, renewing its bid to regain control and pull Jim back into his comfort zone.

Your subconscious mind acts just like a child and soon gets bored.

Just imagine taking a five-year-old child to the gym with you. At first they may be excited and full of energy, dragging you around the gym and trying out all the equipment. This might continue for two or three visits, but then the child would begin to get bored and start whingeing about having to go. You would end up virtually dragging them there, and while you doggedly followed your keep-fit programme, the child would probably be sitting in the corner sulking.

This is exactly what happens in reality; only it's your inner child that behaves in this way. You don't realise that this is what is going on; you just feel the symptoms. Your enthusiasm wanes, you feel tired, you look for excuses not to go, and the next thing you know, you haven't been for weeks and you regret taking out a gym membership that commits you to the next – very expensive – six months.

Familiar story? I know it's happened to me on more than one occasion. Yet again, it's the subconscious mind dragging us back into our comfort zone – no wonder it is so hard to go forward in life when the most restricting factor is hidden in our own head. But remember, knowing what's going on is the first step towards being able to do something about it.

Jeff and Dave's stories

Another way to explore the notion of the comfort zone is to compare two people with similar upbringings. Jeff and Dave had known each other all their lives. They grew up together on a housing estate in a typical working-class environment. Their birthdays were only three days apart, and as children they were inseparable.

Jeff was the youngest of five children, with two brothers and two sisters. Life was quite hard for them, as their father and mother had separated when Jeff was only five years old, and during the time before the separation the house had been filled with arguments and anger as his parents struggled to cope. Jeff's father had never held down a job for long and spent most of his time drinking and gambling away the family's money on the horses. Money was therefore scarce, and Jeff had to rely on hand-me-down clothes from his older brothers. The family always had enough to eat, but there was no money for life's luxuries, such as holidays, treats or days out. All these factors combined to mean that the primary emotions surrounding Jeff in his formative years were anger, worry, self-pity, hostility, fear and a general sense of having less than everybody else.

As you will now recognise, all these emotions are low-vibrational. Naturally, they contributed hugely to how Jeff felt about himself. He felt that he wasn't as good as most of the other children because they seemed to have lots more than him, so his habitual thought patterns about himself were low-frequency: 'I don't deserve', 'I'm not as good as other people' and 'I can't do anything' were the kind of statements he would unconsciously repeat to himself. This negativity became Jeff's norm. His subconscious mind believed this was what he deserved to be, and it set about ensuring that this was what he got for the rest of his life.

Jeff was a very good soccer player and made the school team, but he found it hard to motivate himself and missed many chances of furthering his progress. He was quite bright but somehow could never be bothered to try hard enough, so he failed most of his exams. He could have made the swimming team but found an excuse so that he didn't have to take part.

When he left school, Jeff found work with an insurance company as a sales representative. He did okay, but somehow he was never going to be one of the high flyers. After a few years in this job he decided that selling insurance was too much like hard work and that he would do much better in a new job, even though some of the other reps were making good money and doing very well. He always had his own reasons for why they did better than him. It was because they had better areas than him or easier policies to sell. One thing was for sure: it was never his fault. So Jeff continued moving from one job to the next over the next few years, not really getting on in any of them, because – according to Jeff – the other reps always had it better in some way. In the end, he put it down to the fact that he just didn't have any luck.

The crucial fact that Jeff wasn't aware of was that he himself was in control of his seeming lack of good fortune. His subconscious mind – programmed to believe that Jeff

Dave and Jeff had totally different outlooks on life: Dave was positive, Jeff was negative.

deserved to stay at a low frequency level – was monitoring his life all the way along. In order to keep him at his frequency level, it 'allowed' him only a very small amount of success – any more would have pushed him into a higher frequency zone. As soon as it looked as if he might become more successful, his subconscious mind kicked in and sabotaged any possibility of that happening. A little voice in Jeff's head would convince him that somebody had it in for him or he never got a fair chance or he should find another job because nobody in his current company appreciated him. This is how our subconscious mind keeps us within the comfort zone that it is programmed for.

Now let's take a look at Dave. Dave was an only child whose parents doted on him. His father was a foreman at the local steel works and his mother a very loving woman who spent her time looking after the family and their home. Dave's home was filled with love and positive energy. He remembers that his parents very rarely argued or had any kind of disagreement. Dave grew up a very happy child, whose parents gave him lots of attention and constantly told him that they loved him. Being an only child, he wanted for nothing. He always had fashionable clothes, and there were holidays abroad every year.

Growing up in this pleasant, loving, high-vibrational environment programmed Dave's subconscious mind to believe that this was the frequency zone in which he belonged. His habitual thought patterns about himself were positive: 'I know I can do it', 'I deserve the best', 'I am as good as anybody'.

Dave was never quite as good at soccer as Jeff, but he worked hard and with conviction, so he progressed further and made it to junior colts level with the local professional soccer club. Dave was not quite as bright as Jeff, but, again, he worked hard and eventually left school with good qualifications. After school, Dave followed Jeff into the insurance business and also became a sales representative. He always came in among the top two or three sales reps in the area. He loved his job, and his attitude impressed the management. He was soon promoted to area sales manager, then a few years later to regional sales director. Dave's life seemed charmed compared to Jeff's; everything always seemed to work out for him.

Jeff and Dave's friendship suffered over the years as their different life paths moved them into different social circles. Of course, they still spoke when they met, but after a while they found they had little in common, and their meetings became more of a passing hello than an in-depth conversation. In fact, Dave's success engendered not a little resentment in Jeff, which, sadly, estranged the two men even further.

Why our vibrational frequency is so important

Looking at Dave and Jeff's lives gives us an idea of how incredibly important our early years are in determining how easy the rest of our life is likely to be. Even though Dave was less talented and not as bright as Jeff, it was still much easier for him to be successful in life than it was for Jeff.

Dave's subconscious programming was of a much higher frequency than Jeff's. His feelings about himself and his own expectations were on a more high-vibrational frequency. He felt better about his abilities, so he had the confidence to try harder; he expected the best, so he impressed others with his positive attitude. All this enabled him to be successful at most of the things that he attempted. His subconscious mind monitored his life and kept him in the higher-frequency zone where it was programmed to believe he should be.

This meant that Dave saw life in a very different way from Jeff. What appeared to be insurmountable obstacles to

*Dave had a much more high-frequency upbringing than Jeff,
and this was the real difference between them.*

Jeff were mere molehills to Dave. In a situation where
Jeff's subconscious mind might say, 'That's just my luck; it
will never work out for me', Dave's would say 'I'm always
lucky; I know this will work for me'. Where Jeff's
subconscious might say 'This job is a waste of time;
everybody has an insurance policy', Dave's might say, 'I
love this job; everybody needs insurance'. At higher
frequency levels, life looks and feels completely different
than it does at the lower levels. Jeff and Dave had exactly
the same job, dealing with the same customers, and they
had the same potential for success; the only difference was
their vibrational frequency.

By now you will have a very clear idea of how our
personal vibrational frequency can control our lives. You
will soon begin to learn how high-vibrational thinking can
help to change that frequency and put us back in control.

Frequency Variations

Before we move on to looking at how to start raising your vibrational frequency, there is one more issue to consider. That is how our average vibrational frequency changes naturally. Although it is true that the foundations of our subconscious, and therefore our average frequency level, are established at an early stage, our frequency level can and does change in relation to time, the people we interact with and the various challenges life presents us with.

We regularly encounter both high-vibrational and low-vibrational energy from both inside and outside. Here we are going to look at the energy we encounter from outside. How we cope with this on the inside is, of course, vital, so we'll look at this issue at the end of the chapter.

Frequency interaction

How we interact with other people has a major impact on our energy levels on a daily basis. In the case of Jeff and Dave in the previous chapter, we saw that Dave had a fundamentally positive, high-frequency energy, and because of this he made other people feel better too. The management recognised his potential, the customers were more responsive. This is because any interaction with another human being affects your frequency level. If you interact with somebody of a higher frequency, you will have your frequency pulled up; likewise, if you interact with a person of a lower frequency, you will be dragged down. This is why some people feel very draining to be with, whereas others feel uplifting.

A positive, high–frequency attitude is great to be around.

It's easy to demonstrate this effect just by thinking about a few of the people you know. If you are having a conversation with someone who is up–beat and enthusiastic, there's lots of high–vibrational energy around. You can chat for hours without the conversation lagging. On the other hand, if you are having a conversation with someone who is withdrawn and unhappy, there's so much low–vibrational energy that you may struggle to keep the conversation going. You are being affected by this person's low–vibrational energies – as they are likewise affected by your vibrational frequency.

Let's pursue this a bit further. If you are yourself feeling down while you are trying to cheer someone else up, it will be much harder work. In fact, it's quite likely that you will both ending up crying into your beer! On the other hand, if you are feeling pretty good at the beginning of the conversation, they may pull you down a bit, but it is more likely that you will be able to raise their spirits and help them to feel better.

The more you can be around high-vibrational energy, the more it will benefit your own energy levels on a daily basis. And if you are constantly around high-vibrational people, then the impact can help to stimulate a long-term improvement in your own energies. You really are fundamentally affected by the company you keep.

Places also have a vibrational frequency to which we react. We all have places that we love and others that we find intimidating or uncomfortable. Some towns feel depressing and unwelcoming, whereas other towns feel upbeat and pleasant. Here, we are simply picking up on the collective vibrational frequency of the people who live in a particular place.

Changing energy frequency levels

As we progress through our life, we may find that we achieve success in different things – perhaps our career takes off and we become very good at what we do. This increases and reinforces our good opinion of ourselves, giving us more confidence in our own ability and changing our personal thought patterns. This increase in positive thought patterns means that our personal energy frequency rises. A similar, negative, effect can occur if you have a run of bad luck. If you find the problems you encounter too much to cope with, they are likely to depress your vibrational level.

We all experience natural vibrational fluctuations on a daily basis as we encounter and have to cope with life's everyday events. We have probably all experienced the feeling of being down in the dumps, when our problems seem huge and we can't see a way around them. If we have an interrupted night's sleep and wake up on a rainy day to news of a traffic jam on our route to work on the local radio, it can make things feel even worse. But with a good night's sleep and a ray of sunshine when you open the curtains next morning, you feel a new surge of energy and yesterday's problems diminish. What is happening is that we are simply viewing the same situation from a different frequency level.

Anna's typical day

Let us imagine that during any given day we have 100,000 thoughts going through our mind. These thoughts are influenced by day-to-day activities – people we meet, situations we encounter, whether our favourite team wins or loses, news in the newspapers and so on. The thoughts we have may be high-vibrational or low-vibrational, and each one has an influence on the vibration rate of our personal energy field, speeding it up or slowing it down as we go about our daily activities. Let us take a look at a typical day to give you an idea of how it works.

8.00 a.m.
It's a bright spring morning, the sun is shining, and it feels great to be alive. As Anna throws back the curtains, the sun's rays cascade into the bedroom, illuminating everything in a golden glow. This is one of those days when

she feels on top of the world. The children are relaxed and happy as they get ready for school. Anna's thoughts are **high-vibrational** and she feels content. Her mind is untouched by any of the **low-vibrational** situations that we all encounter every day. At this point of the day, it's fair to assume that her personal energy field is vibrating at a fairly fast rate.

8.30 a.m.
This is a great start, but – hang on – little Lucy is lagging behind and holding everybody up. 'Come on, Lucy. Hurry up or you will be late for school,' shouts Anna. A slight feeling of frustration sweeps over her. This is a **low-vibrational** emotion, and it slows Anna's personal energy field down slightly.

9.00 a.m.
'But it's still a great day,' Anna thinks to herself as she ushers the children into the car and sets off for school. A few jokes on the way ensure a happy and laughter-filled journey so, as this is a **high-vibrational** situation, it speeds up her personal energy field.

9.30 a.m.
The children are safely in school when up strolls Mrs Johnson. 'Oh, no!' Anna says to herself, 'who is she going to be gossiping about today?' Sure enough, away she goes: 'Well I don't know who she thinks she is …' and 'What they need a big car like that for I don't know …'. Now Anna's personal energy field is slowing down as she lends a sympathetic ear to Mrs Johnson and listens to her jealousy, resentment and envy directed at one person after another. The **low-vibrational** conversation is dragging down Anna's energy field. After 15 minutes, Mrs Johnson announces that she has to go, leaving Anna slightly dazed and feeling decidedly grumpy.

Anna's vibrational level is lowered by contact with another person's negative energy.

10.00 a.m.

The journey home is uneventful; a good thing really, because Anna is in no mood for any aggravating drivers. After parking the car, she opens the front door to find a pile of letters waiting for her on the carpet. 'Let's see what we've got here then,' she thinks to herself. 'Gas bill, electricity bill, telephone bill, credit card bill and a couple of junk mail letters. Well, there shouldn't be too much to worry about there.' She decides to make a cup of tea before opening the mail.

First, the gas bill: it's slightly more than she was expecting, but their budget can cope with it. 'I wonder if we have a gas leak? No, we probably left the heating on more than I realised,' she thinks to herself. Suddenly **low-vibrational** thoughts begin to creep into her mind, and she starts to worry, so slowing down her personal energy field.

Next, the electricity bill. That's a lot lower than she expected, which is a nice bonus that makes up for the gas bill. She feels a little uplift, and a small wave of **high-vibrational** joy sweeps through her mind. Up goes her personal energy field.

Next, the credit card statement: not so bad!

But then she opens the telephone bill: £500! 'My goodness, how can that be?' Anxiety takes hold as she scrambles around for the itemised statement. 'I knew it! The Internet! I'll swing for him when he gets home!' A flood of **low-vibrational** emotions hit: worry, fear, anger. Anna's personal energy field plummets as she engages in this **low-vibrational** energy. By now, her personal energy field is slowing right down and she feels terrible. That's all she needed; now she has a headache as well.

11.00 a.m.
Anna spends the rest of the morning fretting over her financial problems and feeling very low indeed. 'Will anything ever go right?' she wonders? Suddenly her **low-vibrational** state is interrupted by the doorbell. As she opens the door, Anna is greeted by a big smile from Jane, her next door neighbour. 'Put the kettle on,' says Jane as she charges by, brimming with confidence and **high-vibrational** energy. 'You look fed up,' she says, catching Anna's miserable face. 'What's wrong?' Well, that's just what Anna needed, and she begins to pour out all her problems. As she fires each one towards Jane, Jane just bats it away with her usual **high-vibrational,** positive outlook. After an hour's conversation, Anna feels decidedly better. Jane has put her problems in perspective, and Anna's personal energy field has shot up. The **low-vibrational** thoughts that weighed heavily on her mind an hour ago now seem trivial, and strangely enough her headache has gone as well. Jane dashes off to her mother's, and Anna decides it's time to do the shopping.

Anna's vibrational level is raised by contact with another person's positive energy.

12.00 noon

The sun is bright (although Anna had failed to notice it during her **low-vibrational** morning). She soon has the car backed out of the drive and is heading towards town. She pulls into the car park. Everything seems rosy again, and her stressful morning feels like a distant memory. Her first stop is the butchers; she joins the queue and waits to be served. The butcher is always very friendly. As soon as he sees Anna, he remarks that she looks younger every time he sees her. Anna feels herself blush, but she is very pleased to receive the compliment and feels uplifted. The **high-vibrational** energy directed towards her has pushed up the frequency of her personal energy field, which also has the effect of making her feel good about herself: more **high-vibrational** thoughts, which drown out any **low-vibrational** thought patterns she normally carries about herself.

12.30 p.m.

Soon the shopping is done, and Anna heads back to the car park, laden down with bags. As she approaches the car, she hears a loud screeching noise heading towards her. She turns to see a car hurtling by at speed. It narrowly misses her, but she drops one of her bags of shopping – eggs, tins and fruit fall everywhere. Anna's heart is pounding at the thought of how close the car came to knocking her down – and not so much as an apology. Her initial feelings are fear and panic, but they are soon followed by frustration and anger. She is fuming! 'How could that idiot drive like that?' she thinks to herself. 'What if the children had been with me?' She decides to report the incident to the police. By this time her personal energy field has plummeted as a result of all this **low-vibrational** energy.

*Anna's vibrational level plummets as a result of
stress and anger.*

2.30 p.m.

After two hours in the police station, Anna is feeling very fed up. The possibility of anything being done about the incident appears to be nil. Anna trudges out. Her personal energy field is now very slow indeed. To compound the situation, she is running late to pick up the children, so she dashes to the school, feeling decidedly down in the dumps. The children are very well behaved on the journey home, as they immediately sense Anna's bad mood. Once in the house, she chases them upstairs to do their homework while she makes the tea, her mind racing with the day's events. Bills, Mrs Johnson's gossiping, the car park incident ... Anna wallows in **low-vibrational** thoughts. Her personal energy field is slowing down even further. She feels really depressed. 'Why is life so stressful?' and 'Nothing seems to go right' are the kind of thoughts racing around in her head. The children avoid her, as they can see her bad mood has not lifted. Indeed, Anna's mind is pulsating with anger, which she is ready to direct at her husband when he gets home.

Anna prepares to direct her low-vibrational mood towards her husband.

5.00 p.m.

'Hello, darling!' shouts John, as he opens the front door. Anna is ready for him, fired up and angry. As she turns to face him, her mind is racing with what she is going to say, but he stops her dead in her tracks. 'For you,' he says, handing her a dozen red roses. 'I've booked a table at our favourite restaurant to celebrate my promotion! From now on it's only the best for us. My salary has gone up 20 per cent and they've thrown in a company car. Now, what is it you wanted to say?' All of a sudden Anna's anger and fear vanish; the good news from her husband has dissipated her negativity. Suddenly, she is feeling good, and her personal energy field races up. 'It was nothing really,' she blurts out. 'Anyway, let's celebrate! What marvellous news!' The children come running down the stairs – they sense that the atmosphere has changed from **low-vibrational** to **high-vibrational** energy. Suddenly, the house is filled with happiness; Anna's bad day seems like a distant nightmare. How on earth had she allowed herself to get so down?

7.00 p.m.
A short while later, as she lies soaking in a hot bubble bath with a wonderful night in front of her, Anna thinks back over her day and begins to recognise how she became the victim of her own thinking. Every time she allowed a thought to grab hold of her and control her without offering any resistance, she became the victim of all the **low-vibrational** energy that had come her way. But, she realises, she did not have to engage with these **low-vibrational** energies quite so eagerly. If she could have detached herself from them, her personal energy field would not have been quite so affected. She didn't have to take it so much to heart when Mrs Johnson started resenting and envying everybody. She didn't have to let the bills get her down – she and John had always managed to get by. She didn't need to let the feelings of fear, panic, anger and frustration overwhelm her when the car screeched past her in the car park. And she didn't need to mull over all of these **low-vibrational incidents** for the rest of the afternoon, thus slowing down her personal energy field even further.

Anna's energy field

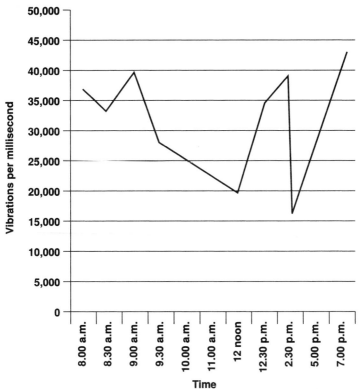

Fluctuations in Anna's energy field throughout the day.

As you can see from the graph, Anna's personal energy field has fluctuated throughout the day as she alternated between positive and negative thoughts – from a low point of 17,000 vibrations per millisecond at 2.30 p.m., when she had just left the police station, to a high point of 48,000 vibrations per millisecond at 7 p.m., as she lay in a hot bath with only positive thoughts in her mind. Remember, the faster our personal energy field vibrates, the better we feel, because we are closer to the high-vibrational energy of love.

Coping with negative energy

It doesn't matter what is pulling you down – the gas bill, the TV breaking down, the children stressing you out. You cannot avoid the low-vibrational energy in your environment; this is the very nature of life. What does matter is how you choose to react to these low-frequency attacks, because you can have some control over how much these situations and events affect you.

I recall an incident in my office in which one of the administrators had had a particularly stressful morning dealing with complaints of various sorts. This low-frequency energy had given her a headache. Then the telephone rang and she found out that she had just won quite a large amount of money. She happily passed on the story of her good fortune to the rest of the staff. A little later, I asked her if she still had a headache. To her amazement, she replied that it had completely disappeared. You see, sometimes even headaches can be instantly cured if you can find a way to lift your personal energy vibration.

On another occasion, a boy I know called Jordan lost his brand-new mobile phone. He was distraught, as his father had just bought him this expensive present. When he realised that he had lost his phone, his whole day looked completely different: one minute he was happy and enjoying himself and the next he was inconsolable. His mind had suddenly become filled with low-vibrational emotions: worry, fear, anger, frustration, disappointment. This had the effect of pulling down his energy frequency. It was several days before Jordan recovered and moved back up to his normal frequency level. That's how powerful negative energy can be.

If negative energy is so powerful, you need an equally powerful weapon to use against it – and that's high-vibrational thinking.

Taking Control

So let's briefly recap. Energy is vibrating all around us. The energy of love is high-vibrational; the energy of fear is low-vibrational. The closer we can stay to the vibration that we call love, the better we will succeed in all aspects of our lives.

Most of life's problems exist at the lower frequency levels, so if you are focused on low-vibrational energy, you are likely to be ill more often, end up in more arguments, have more trouble with your car or your computer, find it harder to get a job or succeed at work, and experience problems at school or with the children. In fact, everything will be much more difficult.

High-vibrational thinking is a way of learning to dismiss low-vibrational thoughts and replace them with high-vibrational thoughts. It makes absolute sense to try to think in a more high-vibrational way, because this puts you in control. And being able to control your thoughts and feelings will help you to change your life. You can learn to use high-vibrational thinking in every aspect of your life. You deserve the positive energies of love, happiness and joy in your life just as much as anyone else.

Just being aware of high-vibrational thinking is the first step to taking control of your energy field, as it enables you to understand what is happening in your mind and to appreciate that control is lacking. Once you have taken that first step, it won't be long before you automatically begin to assess situations in terms of energy and put HVT into practice without thinking about it. This makes a welcome change from being controlled by negative energies, tossed around like a rag doll in the wind.

Reprogramming our subconscious

There are two elements in making HVT work for you: one deals with your fundamental energy levels, and the other deals with how you react to the changing energy levels around you.

The influences we experience during our formative years help to establish our normal vibrational frequency and define our comfort zone: our fundamental feelings about ourselves and the kind of life we believe we deserve. Throughout our life, our subconscious mind monitors our feelings and actions so that we stay within the boundaries of our comfort zone – whether that is good for us or not. If we try to move away from that comfort zone, we are engaging in a battle for control – and it's a battle that we usually lose.

There is another way – one that avoids the battle and enables us to take control. The answer is to re-programme your subconscious mind and so change the boundaries of your comfort zone.

Let's take the dieting example that we looked at on pages 28–9. While your comfort zone is chips, chips and more chips, any diet will be a huge struggle that is almost doomed to failure, because you will be constantly drawn back to your comfort zone. But if you change the boundaries of your comfort zone, your subconscious mind will monitor what you eat to keep you at the newly programmed weight that is now within your comfort zone. You will be able to change your eating habits, with the result that you are attracted to a more healthy diet of less fattening foods. If you look at those people who have dieted successfully and lost lots of weight permanently, you will generally find that they have also successfully re-programmed their subconscious mind.

If it's improved fitness you are trying to achieve, the principles are just the same. While your comfort zone is an evening with your feet up in front of the TV, that is what your subconscious will be pulling you towards.

HVT is a way of re-programming that does away with the need for an iron will. This book will show you how to achieve that re-programming. The first step towards change is to understand how your mind works and accept the power of the subconscious mind. Once you appreciate this, you can begin to move forward and make plans for a new and exciting future.

With HVT you can re-train your inner child.

Of course, once you have re-programmed your subconscious into a new comfort zone, it will start to form new and more positive habits. If you have an established habit of taking regular exercise, when you miss your exercise for some reason, you will feel tired and drained. It's almost as if you are addicted to exercise and without it you feel down. This, again, is your subconscious pushing you to stick to the comfort zone – but in this case, of course, the comfort zone is healthy, so the subconscious is a force for good.

So you can see that your subconscious can be programmed for success or failure, and it will use all its powerful influence to maintain whatever it is programmed for. If we can re-programme our subconscious for success, clearly this is the answer to many of our problems. This book will show you how to do just that – to change your subconscious comfort zone in relation to the specific problems and issues that are relevant to you.

Start changing now

You don't have to wait until you have read the whole book to make changes in your life. You can start making changes straightaway. Start by dealing with the energy fluctuations you encounter on a daily basis and how you react to them.

Remember the outline of Anna's fairly ordinary day (see pages 40–7). Look at it again and you will see how Anna allowed herself to be engaged by the energies around her rather than taking control of her own energy field. When she encountered low-vibrational energy from outside, or when her own emotions were low-vibrational – both things we can't always avoid – she allowed herself to be dragged down and ended up feeling even worse. You are probably just the same. Now that you realise that by engaging with low-vibrational thoughts you are only going to damage yourself by dragging down your personal energy field, you can start to implement changes that will make an immediate difference to your life.

Don't engage with low-vibrational energy

The crucial thing is not to engage emotionally with low-vibrational energy, because it is when you become emotionally attached to negativity that you are most damaged. Your personal energy frequency will plummet and move you into a much more difficult frequency zone.

You can now recognise low-vibrational energy as anything that pulls you down and makes you feel negative: anger, disappointment, envy, spite and so on. When you encounter that kind of energy, the secret is to remain calm and to let the negative energy pass over you without buying into it. Try to visualise the energy moving away from you and disappearing, rather than hanging on to it and engaging with it mentally. The principle is very simple: recognise it and reject it.

Start right now. The next time you find low-vibrational thoughts coming into your mind, let them go. You almost certainly won't succeed straightaway; it will take a little practice, but even the first time you try it, you will feel some impact. Then, every time you succeed, it will become easier and more automatic to reject negativity. If you stick at it and follow the specific guidance in this book, you will get better at it every day.

Take bills as an example. If you have a gas bill that is higher than you expected, you obviously have to do something about it. But worrying is not going to make the bill any smaller; nor is it going to get it paid. If you put aside the worry, you have more energy to think about positive things that will help you to solve the actual problem of paying the bill. Your mind will be able to focus on the options: you can dip into your savings, contact the supplier and arrange to pay it off gradually, turn down the heating thermostat so it doesn't happen again – or whatever.

Concentrate on the present

So visualising negative energy draining away will help. Another very simple way to handle low-vibrational thought patterns is to concentrate on the present.

We all spend too much of our time thinking about the past or the future. Our minds tend to dwell on something that has happened or something that might happen until this becomes a habit that is difficult to break. In fact, we are often scarcely aware that we are doing this.

It is all too easy to dwell on a low-vibrational event that has happened in the past: the time we struggled to meet a payment date; the time someone shouted at us or let us down. We keep running it over and over again in our minds like some kind of loop-tape action replay. The result of replaying thoughts of anger, frustration, disappointment, fear or uncertainty is that our personal frequency level is dragged down even more, pulling us down into a negative zone.

Likewise, we may focus our attention on a future negative event that may never happen: the cold we are sure we are going to catch, the redundancy that is bound to come, and so on. Similarly, the effect is to lower our frequency level, leeching away all our positive energy.

The past is gone and we cannot change it. Dwelling on its negative energies will only drag us down. We simply need to learn from it and move on. The future is not here yet; worrying about something that may or may not happen will only drag down your personal energy field, making life much harder in the process.

If you can avoid this time trap and think in the present, you will find that your energy levels remain high. By being alert to this pitfall, you can train your mind to recognise when you are about to fall into the trap. Then you simply stop and remind yourself to concentrate on the present. If you have a problem, look at what you can do now to solve it in the best possible way.

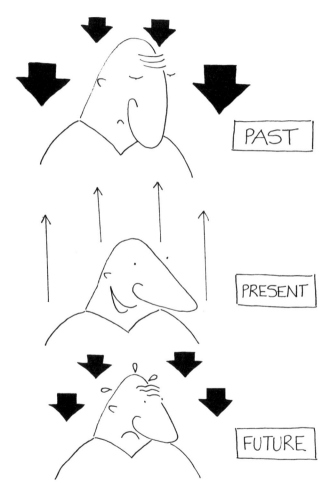

Dwelling on the past and worrying about the future is a waste of energy. Stay focused in the present if you want to get the best out of your life.

Use high-vibrational thinking to clear your mind of clutter and stay focused in the present moment; then you are ready to handle life to the best of your ability.

Take one step at a time

There will be times when you don't manage to dismiss low-vibrational thoughts altogether. Don't worry about it – for worrying is in itself hanging on to low-vibrational energies. Look at what you did achieve; tell yourself how much better you did it than last time; congratulate yourself and move on. Before long you will find that you are more and more in control. This means that your personal energy field will not slow down as easily next time you encounter low-vibrational energy, and you won't have to spend every day on a mental rollercoaster ride.

Remember, you are more in control than you realise. Your thoughts create your reality, so if you fill your mind with high-vibrational thoughts, you will have a more positive, enjoyable and fulfilling life. You can take control of your own energy.

Your Employment Potential

'*We are unlimited beings, experiencing life in a physical body subject to the ceilings of our imagination.*' Bill Hicks (Comedian)

Now you understand how HVT works, you are almost certainly beginning to apply it to your life. Here, we are going to look specifically at how HVT can help you improve your chances of getting a job so you can attack the job market with new vigour and enthusiasm and find work that suits your abilities. The final section of this book offers a complete six-week programme to enable you to put your new-found knowledge into practice in a structured way.

To realise your full potential, you need to attune your personal energy field to the frequency of love on a permanent basis. This means both that your own comfort zone will be high-vibrational and that you will have learned to deal with low-vibrational energies in your surroundings so that you remain in a high-vibrational energy field all the time – or as much of the time as is humanly possible!

Staying in a high-vibrational zone is the goal – and we are all fully engaged in pursuing this, whether we realise it or not because, whatever happens in our lives, we all want to be happy. Indeed, everything we do is focused on this single aim. Our whole life is geared towards this deep-seated desire to be at one with the energy that we call love.

Of course, we have to accept that we live in the real world and we all have to confront and deal with problems to a greater or lesser extent. It is unrealistic to expect total happiness all the time, but it is realistic to aspire to make our life as good as we can possibly make it. We can make things better – much better – for ourselves every day, and we can start to do this straightaway by harnessing high-vibrational thinking.

Judging your potential

Every one of us has unique qualities, strengths and weaknesses. Within us is the potential to use those strengths to the full and minimise those weaknesses, but we will only be able to realise 100 per cent of our potential if we work at it.

Of course, our individual potential is – much the same as we are – completely unique. Only a very few of us have the innate potential to be, say, a nuclear physicist, the Prime Minister of Great Britain or the President of the United States of America. Most of us would be content with much less lofty achievements: we want to be good parents, have a fulfilling relationship, get a satisfying job and progress to a better one. While a few of us may have the potential to be a top tennis or rugby player, many will be happy to achieve a place in a local club team, and yet more will be content to be able to kick a ball round the park on a Sunday!

Are we achieving our potential?

What our individual potential is doesn't matter. What does matter is how close we are to achieving it. The one thing we can be pretty sure of is that 99 per cent of us are not anywhere near to achieving our potential. I know for certain that this applies to me. I am always aware that I could do better in whatever I am doing – there's always a little bit more to reach for. There is huge room for improvement in just about every area of our lives for almost every one of us.

Why do we fall short?

If we are all falling short of reaching our potential in just about every area of our lives, the million-dollar question is why? I think the answer lies in the lack of a simple understanding of the mechanics of how to do better. You don't achieve your potential without working for it; it doesn't happen overnight. But if you don't know the right way to maximise your potential, all the work you put in may be wasted. Put simply, you can expend a lot of energy digging a hole, but if it's in the wrong place, all that energy is for nothing.

High-vibrational thinking offers you a fundamental understanding of what you need to do to maximise your potential. This will help you to do better at home, at work and in your relationships with other people. The result will be that you feel happier and more fulfilled. In short, you'll feel much better yourself.

Breaking out of the Low-vibrational Trap

If you are reading this book, it is probable that you are at a low point. All of us have experienced this feeling at some stage in our life – perhaps due to unemployment, money worries, the loss of somebody close to us or the break-up of a relationship. When such things happen, it is only natural to find it hard to cope with the logistical issues involved, let alone the difficult emotions that can be associated with such events.

How we react to difficult situations

At times of difficulty or trauma, we tend to turn our problems over and over in our mind. When we cannot find immediate reassurance or instant solutions, we will return to the same ground repeatedly, in the hope of finding the relief we are seeking. On an emotional level, this causes us feelings such as anger, frustration, fear, pain, worry, anxiety and self-doubt.

Dwelling on problems in this way causes our personal energy frequency to plummet, so that it is vibrating at the lower levels. When we are down in this zone, even the normal everyday tasks of life can seem hard work, and we may struggle to drag ourselves out of bed. In every respect, we are seriously low on energy.

Even if your energy frequency hasn't dropped this drastically, your attitude to life will probably still be affected. If you don't observe the change yourself, friends may notice that you are acting in a more negative way than usual.

Unemployment can reduce your energy frequency

If you are unemployed, you could be struggling with these low-vibrational energies, and if you are out of work not through choice, there is even more potential for such negative energies to take hold in your life.

Being out of work can have negative implications throughout your life, while having a job helps to make you feel better about yourself.

Indeed, if we don't find a way out of this low-vibrational trap in the long term, it can have a serious negative impact on our lives. In terms of work, it can become difficult to concentrate and certainly very hard to perform well, and it may get increasingly hard to make the effort to find a suitable job. The worse we feel, the more likely we are to be unable to perform well enough at interviews ever to be able to get ourselves back on the road to a job and a satisfying employment future.

In this scenario, any strategy that will improve your opinion of yourself is worth pursuing, because this will raise your vibration rate and ultimately help you to get back into employment.

Break away from self-imposed limitations

Self-imposed limitations can control our lives. Here is an example. I used to work with a salesman – let's call him Sam – whose family had spent their entire lives on state benefit. He had grown up in this environment and regarded it as normal. This became his comfort zone. When he was old enough to get a job, he carried this programming with him, and it was very limiting. Every time he got a job he would find a reason to leave – and reasons as to why it was not his fault. He usually managed to work for about three months before the self-destruct button was pushed and his subconscious programming pulled him back into his comfort zone.

When I first met Sam, he declared that he would be happy as long as he could earn around £150 per week. The first week he did very well and earned double what he was hoping for, then he did even better the following weeks. He was delighted and declared this was the best job he had ever had. Unfortunately, the next week he had various appointments to keep at the dentist's and doctor's and so couldn't put in a full week, and his earnings dropped below target. The following week his car let him down and he had to take his wife shopping one day, so, again, he had a poor week's earnings. Then he had a week off because he needed a holiday, so he earned nothing that week. The next week was a complete disaster, as his car needed a service and he couldn't find a garage to do it, so he spent that week sorting his car out, again earning nothing.

By now the boss was getting a bit disillusioned and spoke to Sam about his record. However, Sam claimed that his poor sales were not his fault, and listed all the reasons why he could not work.

The rebuke from the boss got to Sam, so he talked things over with his wife, and they agreed that he should not be treated like that. He left the job. When I looked at how many weeks he had worked and averaged out his earnings over that time, the total was exactly what he had hoped for: £150 a week.

There are plenty of excuses for everyone. If you look for them, they will keep you firmly rooted in the low-vibrational zone. Things go wrong for all of us, and we have to cope. We have to find ways to overcome our difficulties. Giving in to them simply makes the job of our subconscious mind easier in terms of keeping us within the confines of our comfort zone.

I watched Sam re-enact the scenario described above several times and even explained to him what I thought was going on. He decided not to take the HVT route and, as far as I know, is still earning way below his potential. You, however, will be different!

The Importance of Work

As we have noted, unemployment can be a significant factor in keeping you in the low-vibrational zone – with all the associated negative implications. Work is important to your self-esteem. You need to address the issues that spending time out of work raises before these low-vibrational thought patterns become too ingrained. Of course, the worst-case scenario won't happen to you, because you are already beginning to use your understanding of HVT to change your life for the better!

The importance of getting back into the job market

Now that you have some knowledge about HVT, you will probably be aware of the importance of getting back into the job market sooner rather than later – because the negative thought patterns that often accompany unemployment have the potential to create damage that will affect you for the rest of your life.

I met a chap some years ago who had been out of work for almost ten years for a variety of reasons. During that time, he had tried various jobs but soon lost interest and found an excuse to leave. He always insisted that it wasn't his fault the job did not suit him; it was a difficult boss or the ridiculous hours he was expected to work – or something else along those lines. The end result was that he became virtually unemployable. He got so disillusioned with his inability to hold down a job that he simply gave up. 'Why should I bother to work for only a few pounds more each week than I get on state benefits?' became his argument. 'I might as well stay in bed.'

This attitude caused him a lot more problems than he realised, because it affected not only his ability to get a job but also his entire self-image. It was constantly affirming to him that he didn't deserve any of the good things in life – a decent job, a reasonable income, a good relationship with colleagues – and had all sorts of repercussions throughout his life. His personal energy frequency was held down in the low zone by his continual habit of negative thinking.

The benefits of being in a job go way beyond having somewhere to go each day and receiving some income in return. The positive implications of employment are just as significant as the hugely negative implications of unemployment. You feel that you are making a contribution to society rather than being a burden. Your life has a purpose. You feel a sense of achievement. You are able to use your skills and talents and develop your abilities.

The knock-on effects of low-vibrational thinking

Whether or not you realise it, the negative effects, not of being unemployed in itself but of seeing yourself as an unemployed person, have a huge impact on your life in general. Once you begin to define yourself as a jobless person, you are in danger of becoming trapped in a downward spiral of negative energy. What are the probable results if this happens? Self-confidence will dip, enthusiasm will wane, and the sense will gradually overcome you that the whole situation is hopeless and not worth any effort. High-vibrational thinkers avoid people with those kind of thought patterns, as they find them draining. Low-vibrational thinkers, on the other hand, are attracted to them, because they recognise a common energy pattern – the net result being that low-vibrational people drag each other down.

This pattern was very obvious in the life of my associate Sam. His whole life at that time was in disarray. Shortly after he left the company, he broke up with his wife, lost the family home, took to drinking and began to suffer ill health. He was living life in a low-frequency zone and was paying a heavy price: his self-respect was at an all-time low and everything was going wrong.

But that's not how I feel!

You may be thinking, 'But I'm unemployed and my life isn't in that sort of mess.' Of course, many people do cope brilliantly with a downturn in their employment record, and you may be one of them. If this is the case, it's likely that your normal vibrational frequency is pretty high. In Sam's case, his frequency level was habitually low, and that was one of the primary reasons why he was unemployed. His subconscious was constantly trying to find ways to keep him within his low-vibrational comfort zone. By reading this book and understanding HVT, you are equipping yourself with the knowledge you need to reprogramme your subconscious and prevent yourself from falling into the same trap.

What would getting and holding down a decent job have done for Sam? It would have raised his self-respect, which would have pushed up the frequency of his personal energy field, moving him into a higher vibrational zone, in which his life would have looked completely different. Once positive attitudes had replaced negatives ones, he would have been able to find energy and enthusiasm, which in turn would have led to small successes. Inevitably, small successes increase your self-esteem, which means you can achieve even more. Sam would probably have been less inclined to turn to

drink, would have had a greater chance of saving his
marriage and would very likely have been healthier.

The work ethic

Getting into the mind-set of wanting to be in employment
is the first step towards actually being there. If you
recognise that having a job is good for your life in general,
because it raises your self-respect, then you have made the
first and most positive move.

Don't be deterred by the fact that you are very unlikely
to walk straight into the job of your dreams. Even with HVT,
you have to be realistic! True, it's not always easy to settle
for less than the best, but try to look at the process as a
gradual progression. You have to start somewhere, and even
if that starting point is in a job with a relatively modest
salary or few responsibilities, see it as a beginning – a way of
getting back onto the employment ladder. Once you're back
on track, then you can begin to climb the ladder.

Start now!

All this information should be making it abundantly clear to
you that it is important to make a start on your get-back-
to-work programme as quickly as possible, as this will
prevent any negative thought patterns formulating and
becoming fixed in your mind. The longer you are out of
work, the more likely it is that low-vibrational thought
patterns will become programmed into your subconscious.
Even if you have been out of work for such reasons as
motherhood or illness, in which case there's no reason to
expect your long-term energy frequency to have suffered,
your mind could well resist the idea of returning to work.
This is simply because your subconscious needs to adjust to a
new routine and accept that your comfort zone doesn't just
involve being at home and bringing up a family, for example,
but that it also encompasses being that friendly and
knowledgeable sales assistant in the new high-street store!

Techniques to Help You Make a Start

Ibelieve that HVT sheds a new light on self-esteem and offers a springboard back into the job market.

Learning to think in terms of HVT is the way to a happier and more fulfilling life. Once you begin to look at your life in relation to energy, living it effectively suddenly becomes a less daunting prospect, as you now have the element of control that you previously lacked. HVT will become a way of life for you, as it has already for many people, and the principles of HVT will enable you to handle your life in a much more productive and beneficial way.

This new-found ability will become an automatic response, and you will find yourself changing as a person almost without you noticing it. Many HVT students have realised the impact that HVT has had upon their lives only when they have met up with old friends or relatives that they hadn't seen for some time. These friends and relatives have been astonished at the changes in them and amazed that something so simple can have such a dramatic impact. This, of course, makes the friend or relative eager to learn more. This is how news of HVT is spread. HVT truly is a self-development tool that works – and, once you have made it a part of your life, works with very little conscious effort on your part.

In your case, HVT will help you to get back into employment. Once you are in a job, you will begin to feel you belong among the employed not the unemployed.

The missing piece

My own experience of the many other self-development theories is considerable, as I spent 20 years before I discovered HVT learning about them. While I found many enlightening and helpful, I always felt that something was missing. I believe HVT is that missing piece of the jigsaw and that an understanding of HVT is essential as the foundation of all your other self-development strategies.

The first affirmation

The first step in returning to work is affirming to yourself that you are going to get back to work and you can and will do so if you persevere. Keep reminding yourself that you are going to find that job that you want, you are going to impress the employers at the interview and you are going to feel great when you receive that letter of acceptance. Write this affirmation on a piece of paper and stick it on the fridge door or keep it in your pocket. You can even write it on the back of your hand. Just keep reminding yourself all the time.

Keep away from low-frequency people

The second vital step on the way to a high-vibrational future is to learn to recognise low-vibrational people and avoid them. You now know what to look out for: anyone whose company makes you feel down, lacking in energy or fed up. A person who makes you feel drained when you are with them is sapping your personal energy. People we enjoy being with should make us feel good about ourselves. If someone you are around makes you start to question your own abilities or lose your self-confidence, this is not a good sign.

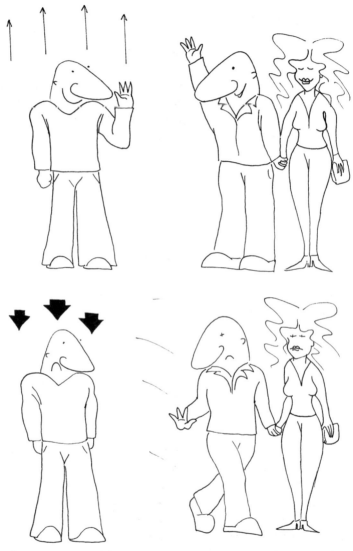

If your energy field is vibrating at the higher frequencies, you will attract other people to you, whereas if your energy field is vibrating at the lower frequencies you will repel them.

Be very careful of so-called friends who seem to be sapping your energy or making you feel depressed or lethargic.

What can you do about this? As far as possible, try to avoid such people. Start to make your own plans. Talk to other, more up-beat people and make arrangements to meet with them. You will find that their high-vibrational energy will help you to build up your own energy levels. It may be difficult at first, so start with small actions that will be effective but not too noticeable. For example, at social events tag along with the lively crowd and make conversation. Each time you score a small victory, it will increase your confidence, raise your energy levels and help you to cope better next time.

Aim for high-frequency places

Places also have energy patterns. A busy factory will be full of energy; a derelict building quite the opposite. Some places feel pleasant, inviting and full of high-frequency vibrations. Others feel depressing, full of foreboding and make you just want to get out. I believe that what we feel when we enter a place is the collective energy frequency of all the people who live or work in that area.

If you live in an area where unemployment is high, the low frequency level of the area will have an effect on you. In general, people will have less money and some may take less pride in their surroundings. You may feel that all of this is within your comfort zone and accept it as normal for you. If so, you will have to work especially hard to re-programme your subconscious. If, on the other hand, you feel uncomfortable in this lower-vibrational environment, your subconscious is already pushing you towards higher achievement levels. HVT will help you to focus on and exploit the positives while avoiding the negatives.

Your home location may be fixed at present, but you don't have to spend all your time in low-vibrational places.

Take yourself to a busy, energising city centre or the calm and quiet of a park, where the energies are healing and positive. But don't make the mistake of thinking that everything and everyone in a high-vibrational place is good – or vice versa. Keep your energy antennae primed for those who are generating positive energy, wherever they are.

Let comments pass you by

There are times when other people's comments can undermine the self-confidence we have built up. If someone makes a negative comment about you – that you are not up to a job, or even something minor like your hair looks a mess – recognise the comment as low-vibrational and let it pass you by. Don't think about it; certainly don't latch on to it and turn it over in your mind. Don't believe it; don't engage emotionally with it. You don't want anything to do with low-vibrational thinking.

Try to imagine such comments as a physical object, perhaps a tennis ball, that is thrown at you but that you can easily avoid by stepping out of the way so that it bounces harmlessly behind you. You may not find this easy to do the first time, but keep at it and it will get easier every time. If a different image works better for you, then use that. You might envisage the negative person as firing a *Star Trek*-style laser stun-gun, while you are protected by an invisible energy shield and the ray bounces harmlessly off you. It's just imagination; anything goes!

Return to sender

Another very effective visualisation exercise to stop other people making you feel negative about yourself is to imagine a huge mirror between you and the other person. If they say something derogatory, imagine that the low-vibrational energy is hitting the mirror and bouncing right back at them.

This visualisation has a double impact. Not only does the mirror protect you from the harmful low-vibrational energy but it also returns the energy to the person who created it so that they have to deal with it. The *Star Trek* laser image works well here too – the offending person has to endure the injury they were trying to inflict on you.

Down in the dumps

A similar principle applies in times when you feel down. We all know that when we are fed up, things look different. Life is bleaker from this perspective. Small problems seem to grow out of proportion; everything feels more difficult to cope with. Then, perhaps after a good night's sleep, a solution is offered, your energy levels pick up and you gain a better sense of proportion. When you are feeling down, try to let go of the negatives rather than hanging on to them. Concentrate on keeping on moving ahead. Life will go much more smoothly for you and your self-esteem will remain higher than if you give in to negative thinking.

Stand up for yourself

Once you have started to use the techniques above, you will soon find your energies increasing. Don't stop there! Keep on telling yourself that you are going to change for the better, and things will keep on getting better. The more you can avoid low-vibrational energy and be around people with high-vibrational energy, the easier it will be to keep your energy field vibrating at the higher levels. Then you are really in charge!

When you have gained a little more confidence, start to speak up for yourself. Don't be frightened to state your opinion; you have just as much right to your view as anyone else. Practise telling people what you think. Enjoy it when they notice a change in you and are impressed that you are speaking up.

Turn the conversation on its head

Another useful technique is to practise changing the direction of a conversation if it is making you feel down in any way. You can learn a lot about this from politicians on television! If the interviewer asks them a question they don't want to answer, they just start talking about something else. If you are with people who you feel are draining you of your high-vibrational energy by talking about negative subjects, being critical, moaning or pouring out all their problems, don't let them do it. Instead of listening to their negativity, interrupt politely and start talking about something more positive.

Stand tall and smarten up

It may sound odd, but you can actually use your physical stance and appearance to help you feel better about yourself. Try this experiment. Think about yourself in your oldest gardening clothes, with no make-up on (assuming you wear it!), your hair in a mess and a spot on your chin. How does that make you feel? Now smarten yourself up in your mind: your best clothes, newly washed hair and a big smile. See yourself standing up tall, with your chin up and your shoulders back. Take a few deep breaths in and out. Feel better? That's not just who you *could* be; that's who you *can* be now!

Take that extra bit of care about your clothes and appearance. You don't have to try to be a fashion icon; just make sure your clothes are clean and tidy. Clean your fingernails and wash and brush your hair. Look at yourself in the mirror and tell yourself how good you look. It's all about raising those energy levels, and small things like this count. Stand tall, look people in the eye and breathe deeply. It will make a real difference.

Let Go of the Past

Putting all these techniques into practice will have slowly but surely built your self-esteem by encouraging you to think in high-vibrational ways. If you now recognise that one of your problems lies in a naturally average energy frequency being dragged down because of circumstances in your past, now is the time to let those circumstances go. If you are lucky enough not to have had a major challenge in your life, then that's fine; you can move on to committing to your back-to-work programme (see page 103).

Today is the first day

Everybody faces certain challenges in their lives, and these can take many different forms – a difficult childhood, a serious accident, a divorce, the death of a loved one, the loss of a job, being bullied at school, parental divorce while you were young. Indeed, no-one's life challenges will be exactly the same as anyone else's. For our purposes, however, their nature does not matter; what does matter is how we handle them. We can either allow them to destroy us or we can fight back and let them be the making of us. It's a simple choice.

If you hold on to the low-frequency events in your past, they will drag down your personal energy frequency permanently, and you will never be free to move into that high-vibrational zone where you feel really good about yourself. You must let go of all the low-frequency energy associated with your life so far, as you cannot move forward until you have made this decision.

The emotions surrounding your life challenges

Think carefully about all the events in your life that you see as challenges and then list them. These might include:

▸ An unhappy childhood
▸ The loss of a sibling or parent
▸ Being bullied
▸ A parental divorce
▸ Losing your job
▸ Failing an important exam
▸ A divorce

When you have completed your list, write down all the low-vibrational feelings you associate with these events, such as anger, hatred, self-pity and so on. Remember, these are the low-vibrational thoughts and feelings that are damaging your life. When your list is complete, you will be able to see the negative feelings and emotions that are causing you the most problems, and this will help you to be more aware of them the next time they occupy your mind.

Events	Emotions
....	....
....	....
....	....
....	....
....	....
....	....
....	....
....	....
....	....

Events	Emotions
....	....
....	....
....	....

When you do encounter these emotions again – and you will – recognise them and step back from them. Tell yourself very firmly that these are low-vibrational emotions and that you do not want to engage with them any more. We will talk more about how to do this in the next chapter.

Forgiveness

Look at your list and make a commitment to forgive anybody who you feel may be responsible for your challenge. You need to do this because, as you now know, holding on to hurt and bitterness can only damage you, and your personal energy frequency suffers as a result. Resentment is a low-vibrational energy; it cannot benefit you. Let it go.

Why this will set you free

If we take a look at all of this in terms of HVT, it becomes a lot easier to understand. Let's take, for example, somebody who had a difficult childhood in which one or both parents were unemployed. When they themselves left school, they received little encouragement to find a job. A person from this background would be likely to have a low opinion of themselves, and their subconscious would feel comfortable with the fact that they did not have a job. This is the kind of negative patterning that can become imprinted on their mind and will constantly circulate to become their subconscious programming – their comfort zone. It is easy to see how years of living with these kind of habitual thoughts will keep their personal energy frequency vibrating at the lower levels and prevent them from finding and keeping a good job.

This is why accepting and letting go of the past is so important. It is the key to releasing the negative thought patterns that are so tremendously damaging. It is vital to forgive anybody you may be holding responsible for your current situation. Remember, they too were subject to the limitations of their upbringing and also had to face challenges in life. Let go of any low-vibrational thoughts and move forward into your future.

The secret of now!

If you are thinking that it is difficult to let go of what has happened in your past, you're right! But it is possible. You can do it.

This is where the secret of *now* is so important. Let go of the past – it's over and you cannot change it. Don't worry too much about the future either – it isn't here yet, and, in any event, dealing with the present is the best way to set things to work out for the best. Focus on the present moment and make it as good as it can be. You are fully responsible for your life, and this is your opportunity to take control.

Burn Your Bridges

Burning your bridges means making a very powerful statement of commitment to change, leaving no way of turning back. You are declaring to your subconscious mind that you are focused on your objective and will not consider the possibility of failure. Commitment has the effect of silencing your subconscious mind, cancelling out its low-vibrational chatter and enabling your frequency to rise accordingly, moving you into a much more productive vibrational zone. When this happens, you rise much nearer to your full potential, and you will be amazed at what you can achieve.

Historic proof that it works
There is a famous story about Ulysses. On arriving at Troy he found his army vastly outnumbered by that of the Trojans and ordered that all of his ships should be destroyed. He then declared to his army that they must return home in their enemy's ships or face certain death. Against all the odds, they defeated the Trojans and returned home victorious.

By leaving no way back, Ulysses made a very powerful statement not only to his own army, whose lives now depended on victory, but also to the Trojans. If the Trojan army had any doubts about the conviction of their opponents, they were surely quashed.

Burning your bridges commits you to your objective.

Muhammad Ali was a great exponent of burning his bridges. He often predicted his own victory in a very public way and even stated the round in which he would win. This committed him to his objective and cast doubts in the mind of his opponent. Doubts, of course, are negative thoughts that pull down the frequency of the person entertaining them, moving them into a lower-frequency zone. This impairs their performance, giving an advantage to their opponent.

How you can make it work for you

When you are starting to look for a new job, make sure you tell all your friends what you are doing and how you are going to succeed. You will be seriously motivated if your willpower begins to weaken.

It helps to be specific when you are setting yourself targets, but there is more than one way of doing this. For

Leave no avenues of escape and your subconscious will be much more likely to help you.

example, you could set yourself the target of finding a new job within six months, or of asking your boss for a rise. Alternatively, you could set yourself a negative target, for example declaring that you will never again agree to complete a job that someone else should do when in reality you have less time than the other person.

It takes a lot of strength and courage to burn your bridges, but it is a very effective way of committing yourself and it helps close the door on self-doubt and the low-vibrational energy that is always ready to creep in and drag down your personal energy frequency.

Don't Open the Door to Doubt

To achieve peak performance in anything, we have to be totally committed and believe 100 per cent that we can do it. Doubt leaves the door open for low-vibrational energy to creep in and pull down our personal energy frequency, which means that we are falling short of our potential. The more intense the low-vibrational thoughts, the further we fall short of our potential.

Will you find a job? Yes!

Let's say, for example, you are going for an interview. As you arrive at the offices, you see two other people walking in. Both look really smart and efficient. The first thought that goes through your mind is, 'They're much more likely to get the job than me.' This opens your mind to doubt, and in floods the low-vibrational energy. Suddenly you feel a little less confident. You begin to entertain thoughts such as, 'I hope this isn't going to be a waste of my time' or 'I knew I shouldn't have bothered'. You just know your personal energy frequency has plummeted, and that only makes things worse. By the time it's your turn to be interviewed, you are in a low-vibrational zone way below your potential, which means, of course, that you have far less chance of getting the job.

Now let's look at the same scenario from a different – high-vibrational – perspective. You see the same two people going into the building, but you are determined that this is the job you want, so you think, 'They must be over-qualified for this job. I'm far more suited to it than they are, and I can prove to the interviewers that I am really hungry for the job.' This kind of thinking raises your personal energy frequency slightly, moving you into a higher frequency zone and increasing your potential to perform well at the interview and get the job.

If we really believe in ourselves and are convinced we can succeed, then we will give ourselves the greatest possible chance of success. If we hold on to high-vibrational thought patterns and shrug off low ones, we will feel better about ourselves, achieve more and be happier.

Your Back-to-work Strategy

Once you have started using HVT to help change your mind-set, you are ready to put your new-found energy into practice. After all, you won't find a job by just sitting and thinking about it!

This chapter will help you to hone your back-to-work strategy with some practical ideas. It's not a complete list of tactics by any means, but hopefully it will point you in the right direction and get you generating ideas of your own.

Find your strengths

Make a list of all the things you are good at. They don't have to be work-related – although if you think hard enough, you will find that most of them have an employment application somewhere. Include anything – anything at all – that you see as a strength in your character. Here are some ideas to get you going:

- ▶ Honest and trustworthy
- ▶ Caring and sympathetic
- ▶ Strong and athletic
- ▶ Intelligent
- ▶ Good with figures
- ▶ Get on well with people
- ▶ A good eye for detail
- ▶ Tidy and well organised

Now write your good points in the left-hand column below.

I'm good at   *Job ideas*

....
....
....
....
....
....
....
....
....
....

Look at the right-hand column. Jot down any jobs you
think fit the strengths you have identified. It doesn't matter
if they are totally irrelevant to your circumstances and
lifestyle. If you are 55, slightly overweight and get out of
breath when you run for the bus, you can still put down
international rugby player on the right if you have written
strong and muscular on the left. This is an exercise in
lateral thinking. The purpose is just to get the ideas
buzzing around in your head and to make you think
positive, high-vibrational thoughts in a work context.

Don't ignore your weaknesses
You don't want to play up your weaknesses, but you do
need to acknowledge them honestly. You may want to be a
professional dance teacher, but if you have two left feet,
you are setting yourself up to fall before you even start
– quite literally!

Sit down and make a list of your weaknesses – perhaps,
for example, you tend to be a bit untidy, you are lacking in
concentration or you are somewhat unfit. Now jot your
weaknesses down in the left-hand column overleaf.

I'm not so good at	*How can I improve?*
....	....
....	....
....	....
....	....
....	....
....	....
....	....
....	....
....	....
....	....
....	....
....	....

Turn to the right-hand column. Now think about what you can do about these weaknesses. For example, you could get up ten minutes early and walk to the shop for a paper every morning to boost your fitness levels. You might decide to keep your bedroom tidier. Jot down anything that will help to eliminate your weaknesses – or at least mitigate them! Taking this action will help to raise your energy frequency because you will know that you are increasing your job potential.

What are your skills and qualifications?

The next step is to identify any specific skills and qualifications you have that will help you in the job market. If you have GCSEs or other educational qualifications, write them down. If you have technical skills, such as an IT qualification or certificate of attendance, put that on your list. If you have done a football coaching course or attended a course to qualify you to help at playgroup, put that down too. Then, once again, write down your skills and qualifications in the left-hand column on the next page.

Skills and qualifications	Job ideas
....	....
....	....
....	....
....	....
....	....
....	....
....	....
....	....
....	....

Look at the right-hand column and jot down any jobs that spring to mind when you think about the skills and qualifications you have.

Mothers returning to paid employment

A word here specifically for women who have spent some years away from paid employment while bringing up children. Always remember that childrearing is one of the most valuable jobs you can possibly have done. It demands selflessness, physical energy, imagination, organisation, creativity, multi-tasking – and the determination to put up with all the boring bits like the washing, the shopping and the housework.

Don't let your natural apprehension hold you back – because you will almost certainly be feeling apprehensive! Your comfort zone may have been established at a perfectly healthy high-vibrational level when you were a child, but being out of the paid-work routine will have altered what you are used to and how you view yourself. The way to change this is to use all the techniques in this book to raise your energy levels. Make sure you take time to focus on paid-work-related activities and don't forget to give yourself full credit for the skills and expertise you have gained as a full-time mother.

What kind of work do you want?

Think about all the aspects of the type of job you are considering. Don't restrict yourself but do think about your priorities, such as how far you are willing or able to travel. Pick some jobs from the lists you made above and imagine yourself actually doing them. Be realistic. Don't go for brain surgeon if you'd make a brilliant hospital porter.

Look in the newspapers and on the internet, go to the job centre or an employment agency. Find out as much as you can about opportunities in your chosen area so that you have a realistic idea about what you can expect.

Remember that you may have to start with something that is not quite the job you want. If so, don't see it as a negative ('This isn't the job I really want'); see it as a positive ('I am on the job ladder and I will do this job well and move on to something even better').

Part-time/full-time

If you have been out of the job market for a long time, you may want to consider looking for a part-time job rather than going straight back into full-time employment. This will have the effect of slowly pushing the barriers of your comfort zone, so that you can gradually re-educate your subconscious mind and ease back into full-time employment.

If you rush back into full-time employment before you are ready, you are more likely to find that your initial energy and enthusiasm wane after a few months and your subconscious programming re-asserts itself and tries to sabotage your efforts.

Keep yourself in a high-vibrational mindset

Keep telling yourself that you can and will succeed. Don't miss any opportunity to visualise yourself in a successful interview or a job you enjoy. Use all your downtime to imagine a successful, working you!

Taking the Issue to the Comfort Zone

Before we move on to the six-week programme, let's just remind ourselves what we are ultimately trying to achieve, which is to re-programme your comfort zone so that it works in your favour. Your subconscious mind established a set of rules when you were young to govern what it sees as normal for you, and it is monitoring you to stay within these boundaries. If you suffer from low self-esteem, it is because you feel – for whatever reason – that you don't deserve any better.

This may be because you were put down as a child by a member of your family and have grown up to accept this as normal. It may be because you have suffered a traumatic event. All that is necessary is that your subconscious starts to consider this as normal for you, and the next thing you know it becomes your comfort zone. Once that has happened, you begin to affirm to yourself that this is where you belong with low-vibrational thought patterns concerning yourself and your environment.

The power of the subconscious

Let's look at an extreme example to clarify how this works. We have all heard about, or perhaps know, people whose lives have fallen apart; perhaps they are addicted to alcohol or drugs or are indulging in anti-social behaviour. How have they ended up in this situation?

Even a minor negative event, if it is repeated sufficiently frequently in childhood, may be enough to establish in a person's mind that they are deserving only of a limited amount of success in their lives. Once their subconscious accepts this belief, their behaviour is almost guaranteed to make sure they get only the worst. They will tend to avoid work at school, get into the wrong crowd, and accept negative criticism and live up to it. In short, the cycle of low-vibrational energy in their life will spiral downwards – with disastrous consequences.

Once you are in that cycle, it is very difficult to break out of it. But it is not impossible. With the help of HVT anyone can reach an understanding of what is happening and put a stop to it.

Your subconscious mind will try to convince you that you are content being out of work; it is simply trying to keep you in the comfort zone.

Your subconscious mind is so powerful that what it expects to happen in your life more than likely will. So if you want to turn your life around, you need to re-programme your subconscious to break away from low expectations and open up your employment horizons to encompass the wealth of opportunities that are waiting for you.

Work can give you self-esteem

I meet a lot of people in the course of my work. One girl I chatted to had found herself in the unemployment trap. She told me that her father was always in and out of work, so she knew all about managing on little money, claiming benefits and the associated problems. When she left school, she didn't try very hard to get a job and laughed at friends who were working hard for not much money. She worked sporadically, but her low-vibrational attitude to employment let her down and she didn't last long. Very soon the gap between her earnings and those of her friends had grown considerably. A gap grew up in other ways, too. With her friends enjoying the high-vibrational energy associated with doing a good job, getting a regular salary and relating to work colleagues on a daily basis, she felt very much outside what she saw as an exclusive club. She got in with a crowd of unemployed youngsters with whom she felt comfortable and not threatened.

However, this young woman had the intelligence to realise that as a long-term strategy this was not going to do her any good. She discovered the high-vibrational thinking courses that I run, plugged into the concept of HVT, took all the lessons on board and, by working hard and with determination, managed to turn her life around.

You are worth it!

Tell yourself that you are just as employable as anyone else – and keep on telling yourself. Write it down, post it on the wall, jot it down in your notebooks. Don't miss any opportunity to tell yourself that you are valuable, you can do a good job and you are going to find one. There's any number of ways you can do this, but specific statements usually work best, as they will be more believable.

Try some of these ideas. Tell yourself:

▸ I am smart and stylish.
▸ I am a brilliant cook.
▸ I am great at football.
▸ I am a kind and caring person.
▸ I am hard-working.
▸ I am logical and organised.
▸ I am committed and determined.
▸ I am trustworthy.
▸ I am great with people.

Keep on at yourself all the time, remarking on every small success. You'll be surprised at how quickly they mount up and how much high-vibrational energy you generate with each compliment.

Run through it in your mind

Let's imagine that you are going for a job interview. It's important that you prepare for it in your mind. See yourself having a shower, doing your hair and putting on your smartest clothes. You plan your route to the interview venue, make sure you get there on time and walk confidently into the offices. You smile, introduce yourself calmly and clearly to the receptionist, and breathe deeply and think about what you are going to say as you wait. When you meet the interviewer, you offer your hand and smile.

Continue running the interview through in your head, seeing yourself giving clear and sensible answers. Remember, if you visualise a smooth and impressive interview enough times, this is exactly what you will deliver. When you go to the actual interview, your personal energy field will be vibrating higher, you will feel more confident and you will be far more likely to succeed.

Re-evaluate yourself

Think about the various areas of your life and what you would like in them. Don't go over the top; be realistic. But don't accept negative ideas either. Try to cover all aspects of your life. Once you have a list of about 20 things, type or write it out neatly and pin it somewhere where you can see it every day. If you don't want anyone else to see it, keep it under your pillow and look at it night and morning.

Here are a few ideas to get you started:

▸ I will have a secure job as a mechanic.
▸ I will have a holiday in the sun every summer.
▸ I will be promoted in five years.
▸ I will increase my social circle.

Keep reminding yourself of these goals and telling yourself that you deserve to – and will – achieve them. They are within your grasp. Eventually, your subconscious will get the message and move the boundaries of your comfort zone to a better and more rewarding position.

Don't Let Your Subconscious Drag You Down

After all this hard work, you deserve the success you are surely going to achieve, so once you have found a job, keep your guard up and don't backslide into your old ways, in which you lacked confidence and energy.

Generally, your initial enthusiasm and excitement at the thought of starting a new job gives you the energy and determination to override your subconscious. After about three months, however, you may find that your subconscious programming starts to fight back. You may feel tired and unmotivated, with your head full of valid reasons why you should not continue to work. These are all sure signs that your subconscious is making a play to re-implement its old programming. You must remain strong-willed and determined if you are successfully to negotiate the hurdles it is placing in your way. Use affirmations and visualisation to maintain your focus, and keep moving forward, even if it is difficult to do so. This will show your subconscious that you mean business. After a couple more months you will find that you have made permanent changes and your subconscious has accepted the new programming.

Coping with promotion

Another situation that may be challenging is being quickly offered a promotion. Let's say, for example, that you have found a job as an assistant in a retail store, and after six months the supervisor asks you to take on a bit more responsibility. The best way to deal with this is to step up your affirmations and visualisations as you take on the new responsibility to make sure that you adjust to the new comfort zone it requires. If you are aware that your old subconscious programming may be lurking in wait to catch you out, you will then be one step ahead. Watch out for the following thought patterns. They should ring alarm bells:

▸ I'm taking more responsibility but I'm not being paid any more.
▸ The extra pressure is taking its toll on my health.
▸ My family will suffer if I work longer hours.
▸ I'll have less free time.
▸ It will be my fault if things go wrong, and I will be made the scapegoat.
▸ I'm being given the job because no-one else wants it.

These are low-vibrational thoughts – avoid them! Take the new responsibility as a recognition of the good work you have done. If you have a genuine grievance, think about it constructively and then talk to your supervisor to find a positive solution.

A cautionary tale

Some time ago, I interviewed a man for a job. He came across very well at the interview and seemed to be the ideal person for the position; he was well qualified and exuded confidence. He accepted the job and made a good start, and I was pleased with my choice.

Then, about three months into the job, he suddenly

changed – so drastically that he seemed to have become a totally different character. He began to be late for work. He always had some excuse – it was the alarm clock, it was the night before, it was his car, and so on. He became arrogant and overbearing, causing bad feeling and resentment amongst the other staff. His productivity rate dropped, and he didn't do the tasks that were required of him. He developed an attitude of self-importance and appeared to believe he was indispensable. Nothing seemed to deter him from this path of self-destruction, and eventually I had to ask him to leave. He didn't take this very well and carried on trying to cause problems. His inability to take responsibility for his actions had resulted in him losing his job, but he blamed everybody but himself.

When this unfortunate incident came to an end, I thought carefully about what had happened. I saw that it could all be explained in terms of HVT. This man's success at his new job had triggered off a response from his subconscious, which immediately proceeded to sabotage his efforts because it could not cope with his new high-vibrational life. He was, quite simply, programmed to believe that he belonged at a lower vibrational level.

This man knew nothing about HVT. You do. Use your knowledge to ensure that this does not happen to you. You can succeed where he did not.

Three Steps to Fulfilling Employment

The final sections of the book focus on the fundamental issue of raising your average vibrational energy level so you can attack the job market with confidence and determination. It is your action plan for changing your life.

Everyone has the potential to get a job that suits their talents and makes their time spent working – and let's face it, that's a lot of time – rewarding and enjoyable. We can't all love every minute of our work – that's just not realistic – but we can expect to be able to work in an environment and at a level that suits our abilities and commitment.

The aim of the exercises in the remainder of the book is to help you become more high-frequency in your general thinking and eliminate any low-frequency thought patterns that you may have been carrying. This will have the effect of increasing your personal energy frequency, which in turn will push the barriers of your comfort zone. There are three steps in this process:

▸ **Step 1:** accept responsibility for your life
▸ **Step 2:** make the commitment to improve your vibrational level and get back to work
▸ **Step 3:** undertake a six-week programme of practical exercises to re-programme your subconscious mind

Step 1: Accepting responsibility

If you are looking to get back into the job market after taking a period out for valid reasons, you simply need to accept responsibility for making the changes you want to happen in your life. If you are looking for a job because you have been made redundant or have not have been able to find an appropriate job for some time, you have to let go of blaming anyone else for what has happened to you so far (even if a redundancy was none of your doing) and accept the responsibility for changing your circumstances. If you truly believe that you can find a job and are able to raise your vibrational energy levels, you will find a fulfilling job and progress in your chosen career. Only you can achieve that – no-one can do it for you.

Whether you realise it or not, you are fully responsible for everything in your life, even if up until now it is your inner child who has been making most of the decisions.

The act of accepting responsibility for what happens in our lives empowers us. It gives us the control that we need to be able to do something about our situation. If we don't accept responsibility, we are in effect giving our power away and blaming outside factors for what happens in our lives. It is vital to accept the fact that you are in control and can do something to enable you to move forward in a positive and constructive way.

Step 2: Making the commitment

You must be totally committed to changing your life for the better if you really want to move forward and get back into the job market. A very strange thing happens when you truly commit to something – you tap into an extraordinary force that raises your levels of power and control beyond anything you would normally expect.

Step 3: Undertaking the programme

Nothing is achieved without work, but it is not difficult to work through the simple exercises I provide. If you repeat them regularly, they will make a huge difference to your life. In addition to the small steps you have been taking so far, I will take you through some proven and powerful affirmation and visualisation exercises designed to push up the frequency of your personal energy field on a permanent basis.

Your self-improvement programme

The programme for self-improvement I am setting you is to be followed over a six-week period, which in my experience is the optimum period to initiate change. However, I strongly recommend that you repeat this six-week module four times, with a one-week rest period in between each of the six-week modules. This will take you a total of 27 weeks, which is the six months that I personally found cemented permanent change.

This is what you will have to do:

- ▶ Make a statement of your acceptance of responsibility and repeat it as often as you like
- ▶ Make a commitment to getting back to work and repeat it as often as you like
- ▶ Dedicate your commitment to someone special to you
- ▶ Read the high-vibrational affirmation I have provided for each week and then write five more of your own
- ▶ Repeat the week's affirmations ten times in the morning and ten times in the evening every day
- ▶ Use a visualisation exercise every day. I have provided the first three; you need to develop three more of your own

All this should take you ten or fifteen minutes a day – not much when the results will change your life!

Use the timetable on pages 120–6 to monitor your progress, ticking off the exercises as you do them. This will help you to stay focused and bring an element of discipline to your programme.

Accepting Responsibility

If you don't admit that there are things you want to change, you will never succeed in changing them. Once you have accepted responsibility for what is happening in your life, you will have the control to do something about it.

If you have opted to leave work to bring up children or to travel, you will have made a conscious decision to take a break from employment. But if you are trying to change unhelpful work-related behaviour patterns, you need to accept that your work record has been weak up to now because at some level of your subconscious you believe you do not deserve to do any better. If you don't accept responsibility, then you are, in effect, giving your power away and blaming outside forces for what happens in your life. It is vital to accept the fact that you are in control and can do something about your work situation if you are to move forward in a positive and constructive way.

The act of acceptance will also make you aware of a whole host of low-vibrational thought patterns. These flourish in a mind that gives its power away. 'Poor me', 'Why am I so unlucky?', 'Everybody is against me', 'It's not my fault' – we are all guilty of these kinds of thoughts, but it is essential to try to avoid them. They are low-vibrational and serve only one purpose: that is, to drag down your energy frequency, making life much harder for you. So, as you can see, step one is vitally important. You cannot move forward until you have acknowledged that you are responsible for your life.

Your acceptance statement

Think carefully about your decision to accept that you are responsible for your life and put it in writing. This will strengthen your belief. You can either copy the following acceptance statement, filling in the date and your name, or write your own.

From today, the .... of .... 20...,
I, ..., accept full responsibility for my life. I realise that there is no point in holding on to any low-vibrational feelings and emotions from the past.
I release any negative energy that I am holding on to.
From this moment I accept total responsibility.

Now read your acceptance statement out loud to yourself.

Strengthen yourself every day

Repeat your acceptance statement over to yourself several times. As you do so, see yourself letting go of all your low-vibrational thoughts and allowing your energy frequency to rise as you move your life forward into a new and exciting future.

Read through your acceptance statement every morning, as many times as you like, and any time you feel your old low-vibrational feelings creeping back.

Making the Commitment

Being totally committed to raising your energy vibration will give you extraordinary power. The dramatist Goethe wrote:

The moment one commits oneself, then providence moves too. All sorts of things occur to help one that would never have otherwise occurred. A whole new stream of events, all manner of unforeseen incidents and chance meetings, and material assistance come forth which no-one could have dreamt would appear.

Something quite magical occurs when we make a committed decision. When our intention is totally focused, we tap into the incredible power of the subconscious. Normally, the subconscious mind sticks to its comfort zone, placing restrictions on our intentions and achievements. However, when our commitment is total, we seem to be able to override subconscious programming and access our incredible potential. If you commit completely, then the possibility of failure is not even a consideration.

What real commitment can achieve

I remember a story a policeman told me about a car accident he attended one night. A young child was trapped under one of the cars and four burly policemen were attempting to lift the car off the child. They struggled

You must be totally committed to changing your life and determined to have a new and brighter future.

without success; the car was just too heavy to move. Then the mother of the child took hold of the car and lifted it off the child by herself. The policemen looked on in amazement at what seemed impossible. What had happened was that the woman had totally committed herself to lifting the car, and her focused commitment had overridden her programming about what was and wasn't possible.

The act of commitment overrides limitations created by our belief system, by society and by our upbringing and enables us to reach our true potential. Once Roger Bannister had broken the four-minute mile and proved that what had been seen as impossible was, in fact, possible, four or five other athletes broke through the four-minute barrier within weeks.

The deeper your commitment, the fewer problems your subconscious programming will cause you. You must leave no exit strategies, allow no 'maybes' or 'we will see how it goes' attitudes. This is a sure-fire way of guaranteeing failure. You must focus totally on success.

Your commitment

You will find that six weeks is a comfortable time period in which to stay focused on your goal, determined and in control without too much interference from your subconscious.

Think carefully about your commitment to what you want to achieve. Then either copy the following commitment statement, filling in the date and your name, or write your own.

> *From today, the .... of .... 20...,*
> *I, ..., commit to focus on my goal with all my strength for the next six weeks. I will succeed in my desire to carry out the exercises and disciplines required, and I will not fail.*

Now read your commitment statement aloud as many times as you like. Any time you feel your willpower beginning to weaken, refer back to your dedication to reinforce your commitment.

Dedicate your commitment

A good way to reinforce your commitment is to dedicate your goal to somebody special to you, perhaps your son or daughter, your mother or father, or your partner. It also helps if you can put the dedication in writing, so that you can refer back to it in moments of weakness. Write down the name of the person and why you are choosing them for your dedication. This may simply be because you love them, or it may be because you want to be able to be more supportive towards them or because you respect them and want to be more like them.

> *I, ..., dedicate the following six weeks to .... because*
> *..*
> *I will make you very proud of me.*

This act of dedication will help to sustain you when your subconscious starts complaining and your determination and willpower weaken.

Making progress

As I have said, it took me personally six months to make real permanent changes within my life, although this may not necessarily be the case for you. However, it will take some time, and that means plenty of opportunities for your subconscious mind to find ways to sabotage your efforts. Watch out for thoughts that are counterproductive to your goal. I found that my subconscious went very quiet for a couple of weeks when faced with failure; then, when I had become complacent in my focus, it suddenly reappeared and was back to its old tricks!

You will know you are really beginning to succeed when quite suddenly you find that the effort you have had to summon up on a daily basis to push towards your desired goal lessens and perhaps even disappears.

Think what it is like when you first join a gym. Your initial enthusiasm propels you through the first few visits. Then your subconscious starts to get bored and begins to find reasons for you to stay at home. If you persist and become healthier, it no longer recognises the new you as fitting in its comfort zone and tries to keep you at the lower frequency level where it feels you belong. But if you keep going nevertheless, one day you will suddenly realise that you can't face life without going to the gym. In fact, if you don't go, you will probably feel down and lethargic. This is your new comfort zone – and this one is good for you!

This process is one that we go through whenever we wish to make positive changes in our life. The trick is to understand what is going on in your own mind. This will enable you to stay committed to your goal and in control of your subconscious mind. You must show it who is boss.

Your Affirmations

I recommend two main methods for helping you raise your energy vibration: affirmation and visualisation. Both are really simple and so are easy to put into practice. They rely for their power on repetition, and – believe me – they are a powerful way to change your life.

A high-vibrational energy field vibrates faster and expands out much further than a low-vibrational energy field.

The advantage of these techniques is that they can be done in small corners of your day and don't need to impact detrimentally on your routine. If you want to, you can do them quietly on your own and no-one else need be involved. This can be a real help in building up your personal strength and raising your vibrational energy levels in order to help you to get back to work.

Positive affirmations

Affirmations are powerful statements that you repeat to yourself so often that you persuade your subconscious mind to accept them as being true. If you continually bombard yourself with these statements, you will re-programme your subconscious mind, thus redefining the boundaries of your comfort zone. Obviously, you need to use powerful high-vibrational statements, which you can tailor to your own particular needs. This will have the effect of replacing low-vibrational thought patterns with high-vibrational ones and raising the frequency of your personal energy field. The longer you keep this up, the more permanent the rise in frequency will be.

Affirmations have a very real influence on your life, so it makes sense to use them to generate high-vibrational energy.

As we have already seen, your life will run a lot more smoothly at the higher frequency levels, so it makes sense to pursue with vigour any methods you have at your disposal to achieve a higher vibrational level.

Writing your affirmations

Here are some examples of affirmations you might use. You can choose anything that strengthens your purpose and brings positive energy into your life.

▸ I am a really great person.
▸ I have loads of energy and enthusiasm.
▸ I am confident and strong.
▸ I am efficient and well organised.
▸ I work hard and with commitment.
▸ I am in control of my life.
▸ I am a valuable employee.
▸ I am respected by my colleagues.
▸ I work well with people.
▸ I can help others.

Affirmations should be written in the present tense, as if you have already attained them. Don't admit of any doubts when composing them.

You can write your affirmations on flash cards and keep them in your purse or wallet or stick them on your fridge. In fact, place them anywhere you will see them as you go about your day.

Using your affirmations

Each week you will read, preferably out loud, six high-vibrational affirmations. Read them ten times every morning and ten times every night, just before you go to sleep. Use the same affirmations for the course of a week, then move on to the next set of six. Keep repeating your favourite affirmations to yourself all day long whenever you can find the time. After a couple of weeks you will be amazed at how different you feel.

Sometimes, after three to four weeks, you may feel that the affirmations are not really working any more. Don't let this deter you. This is a crucial point, at which you must keep up the bombardment of high-vibrational energy. Your subconscious mind can be very clever and will use all of its persuasive powers to convince you to desist. Do not give in. Keep going. The boundaries of your comfort zone are changing without you realising it. After six weeks you will have made noticeable progress.

At the end of the first six-week period, you may want to change some of your statements before you begin your next six-week course of affirmations.

Believe me, you can't bombard your subconscious mind enough! You should live and breathe high-vibrational thoughts. They will push up the frequency of your personal energy field, changing your life for the better in the process. The more high-vibrational thoughts you think, the more used to them your mind will become. You are drowning out the low-vibrational thoughts, not allowing them to take hold and drag down your personal energy frequency. If you do this enough, your subconscious mind will accept that this higher frequency state is the norm for you, and then this will become your natural state of being. As a result, the transition back into work will be much easier for you, as you will believe you deserve success in your life.

Your Visualisations

Walt Disney said, 'If you can dream it, you can do it.' That's what visualisation is all about.

Visualisation is a powerful tool that you can use to help re-programme your subconscious mind. What you are doing is convincing your subconscious mind that you are capable of achieving the subject of your visualisation. The secret to success in any area of life is to believe that you can do it, or – to be more precise – to make your subconscious mind believe that you can do it. As the real source of your unlimited potential lies within your subconscious mind, this is where your true capabilities lie.

Visualisation can help you to mould your expectations to your advantage.

Belief is the key to success, as to truly believe eliminates any doubts from your mind and moves you into a frequency zone where anything is possible. This is the zone where you are calm, happy and detached from the outcome of your objective (becoming over-involved could open the door to doubt and pull your frequency level down into a less productive zone). The secret is to relax, know that you will succeed and trust in your ability; just enjoy the moment and bask in the high vibrations. Then, almost without thinking about your objective, allow everything to flow naturally. Success will be almost guaranteed.

How to visualise

A visualisation is nothing more complicated than a high-powered daydream! You simply need to get comfortable, relax and give yourself completely to your imagination. Learn to see yourself in positive situations in which you are successful at interviews and in your job – earning praise, promotion and responsibility. If you see yourself as a respected member of the workforce, this will become your comfort zone. Remember, you only have to believe in something to make it a reality.

The key to successful visualisation is your imagination: learn to use it to your advantage. See yourself in successful situations, whether they relate to work, relationships or leisure. The more you use visualisation, the better you will become at it and the easier it will be for your subconscious to accept the visualisation as real. Truly believing something will make it happen.

Your visualisation programme

For this programme, you should do a visualisation exercise every day for the six-week period. The best time is when you wake up in the morning, as this will set your energy levels on high vibration for the remainder of the day. Each visualisation takes about five minutes.

I have provided three visualisations. Use these for the first three weeks and then create a new one yourself for each following week. Visualisation is much more effective if you incorporate things that are personal to you. Include anything that makes you feel good about yourself. Make space in your timetable to devise and write your visualisation exercises.

Comfort your inner child visualisation

Your life is merely a reflection of what your subconscious mind believes you desire. As we have already noted, our subconscious mind is also known as our inner child, because it has all the attributes and characteristics of a small child. As you know, it has an established comfort zone, which is the way it is programmed to think life should be for you and where it wants you to remain.

Comforting your inner child shows them that you love them; when your inner child feels loved, they will be much more helpful to you as you negotiate life's hurdles.

Whether this is good or bad for you is irrelevant, as your inner child cannot differentiate between the two.

Comforting your inner child is beneficial in many areas of your life. It allows you to acknowledge the importance of your subconscious while at the same time letting go of any low-vibrational thought patterns that may have taken root there, perhaps some time ago. When looking to move your life forward, it is important to clear out these low-frequency feelings and emotions, otherwise they will hold you back and hamper your progress as if you were carrying a dead weight.

This exercise can sometimes unearth deep emotional issues from the past. Of course, that is what we are trying to achieve, but if you feel in any way apprehensive about this, it may be helpful to have somebody sit with you the first few times you do this visualisation. Then they can offer support and reassurance if necessary. You might like to have them read through the visualisation first to help you work through it.

The point of this exercise is to see your inner child happy and having fun, and most of all to reassure them that you love them. Loving your inner child will help you to release any deep-seated low-vibrational thought patterns that may be embedded in your mind.

You can adapt the visualisation in any way you like to make it more personal to you.

The stages of the visualisation are as follows:

▶ Read through the visualisation first so you understand what it is trying to achieve and what you need to do.
▶ Get yourself comfortable in a warm room, in a comfortable chair or on your bed.
▶ Close your eyes and relax.
▶ Slowly run through the visualisation in your mind.
▶ Once you have completed the visualisation, lie and relax until you are ready to return to the real world again.

The visualisation

Imagine that you are making contact with your inner child for the first time.

You are gazing out of the window and it is a beautiful sunny day. The sun casts its powerful rays across your garden, and you can see the hills and countryside in the distance. The birds are singing, and you decide to go out for a walk. Then you turn around and, to your surprise, see a small child, about five years old, sitting on a chair in the corner of the room. You look at the child and see that they have their head tilted slightly down and appear a little unhappy.

Suddenly you realise this child is you, just as you were at five years old. It is your inner child. You kneel down, take hold of your child's hand and say to them gently, 'Hello. How are you? I'm here to take care of you. Let's go out for a nice walk.' You notice a smile beginning to spread across your child's face and you stand up and open the door.

You walk out together on this beautiful summer day. You feel your child's hand gently gripping yours. As you walk, you reach down and sweep your child up in your arms, giving them a big hug and a kiss on the cheek. You say to your child, 'I love you very much and I am always here to take care of you.' You see your child begin to smile and you give them another big hug. Your child looks happy now. You give them a little tickle and they giggle furiously.

You put your child down and they run off, laughing. You chase after them. You are both having so much fun as you wander down the country lane.

Enjoying your inner child visualisation
Here is a second visualisation for you to use.

The visualisation

You are sitting drinking your morning cup of coffee, contemplating the day ahead. The sun is streaming into your kitchen. Sitting opposite you on a comfortable chair is your inner child, you at five years old. They gaze at you with a bored look on their face. You wonder, 'What can we do today?'

Then you remember the local school is holding its annual fun day. 'Come on,' you say. 'We're off to enjoy ourselves at the fun day.' You watch a big excited smile appear on your inner child's face at the prospect of the fun day.

You both hurriedly get ready, laughing as you pull on your clothes. You decide to take the dog with you. She jumps up and pulls on her lead, excited to be going out for a walk. Soon you are on your way.

The fun day has lots of roundabouts and side stalls, a parade and a motorcycle display team. Your inner child is deleriously happy and loves the rides. You enjoy watching them having so much fun.

You pick up your inner child and hold them close, telling them how much you love them. Then you kiss them on the cheek. The dog jumps up, wanting some attention, and your inner child giggles delightedly at her antics.

Then it's on to the roundabout, with all of you spinning around and having a wonderful time. Your inner child is so happy enjoying all the fun and games. Again, you cuddle them and tell them how much you love them.

You buy three ice-creams, as the dog loves ice-cream, too. It tastes delicious. Your inner child has ice-cream all over their face. You are all happy and full of joy.

After a wonderful day, you set off home with a beautiful feeling of contentment, looking forward to your tea and a nice relaxing bath. Your inner child is happy, and you feel on top of the world.

Getting back to work visualisation

This visualisation relates specifically to attending a job interview. It is particularly important that you personalise it to suit the type of job you are looking for. Use it to see yourself as a person who can choose virtually any job they want. Remember, you just have to believe in what you desire to stand a chance of making it a reality.

Visualise yourself as successful at your job and this is what you will be.

The visualisation

It is a sunny morning when the alarm clock wakes you. You get up, shower and get dressed for your ten o'clock interview. You have plenty of time, so you enjoy your breakfast, then set off for the bus stop, picking up a newspaper on the way.

The bus is right on time, the driver is friendly and chatty, and there's plenty of room, so you don't have to stand. There's a fair bit of traffic, but you are not held up, and you are sitting next to someone going on a shopping trip into town who is happy to chat about the weather and the latest news.

You arrive at the offices and introduce yourself at reception. You have ten minutes before your interview is scheduled to start, so there is plenty of time to visit the bathroom before you are called in. There are a few other interviewees waiting, but you feel confident that you look smart and are well prepared.

The interview begins with an outline of the job specification – it sounds exactly what you want. When asked to talk about your qualifications and abilities, you speak clearly and concisely about what you can do. The interviewers are clearly impressed that your attributes so closely match those they need for the job. You remember to ask a couple of targeted questions before you shake hands and leave. The interviewers' final comment is that they will let you know their final decision within five working days, but that they will certainly put you on the shortlist.

You take the bus home feeling confident in your abilities and quite sure that you will be offered this job.

Visualisation in daily life

Now that you understand the concept of visualisation, you will probably want to use it in your daily life.

You might, for example, set aside five minutes each day to visualise how you want your day to go, putting negative thoughts out of your mind and imagining the best scenario. You might want to run a specific event through in your mind, seeing it with a positive outcome, or you might want to use visualisation to improve your relationships either at work or in the social sphere. Use your imagination to play out any scene that you feel it will help. See yourself and your colleagues in constructive and professional situations – and remember you have to truly believe in what you want in order to begin to make it happen.

Practice is crucial here. The more often you visualise, the more readily your subconscious mind will accept your visualisations. This will enable you to run through any work-related visualisations that you feel may be appropriate whenever you need them, as practice will have honed your skills, making your subconscious mind open to your suggestions. Visualisation puts you in the driving seat, enabling you to control your subconscious mind rather than it controlling you.

As you use HVT in your life, you will become increasingly aware of the constant tussle taking place between your conscious and your subconscious mind. When you notice this taking place, it may help to spend a little time explaining to your subconscious mind what it is that you are trying to achieve. Make your inner child part of your life and remember that your life will be a lot easier if you can enlist their support in your endeavours. Explain to them the benefits to both of you of what you are doing. Don't forget they are a child and make it attractive to them. For example, if you are a student taking exams and feeling unsure of your capabilities, ask your inner child to help you. Explain that if you pass your exams, you will be able to get a better, higher-paid job, which means more treats, such as a trip to the zoo or a new computer game. Remember, you are trying to motivate a five-year-old child, so think in terms of what they would like.

Learning to communicate with your inner child is crucially important if you are really to move forward and fully realise your amazing potential. After all, it is the thought patterns that are programmed into the mind of your inner child that dominate your life. In order to make changes in this area it is vital first of all to open the channels of communication.

My Progress Back to Work

Use these pages to write your own affirmations, make notes on your personal visualisations and tick off when you have completed your tasks. It will help to keep you on track, give you focus and purpose, and also reassure you that things are improving all the time.

My acceptance statement

. . . .
. . . .
. . . .
. . . .

My commitment statement

. . . .
. . . .
. . . .
. . . .

My dedication

. . . .
. . . .
. . . .
. . . .

Week 1
My affirmations

▶ I love and approve of myself.

▶ . . . .

▶ . . . .

▶ . . . .

▶ . . . .

▶ . . . .

My visualisation

▶ Comfort your inner child visualisation (see page 115).

My checklist

Day	Morning affirmations	Visualisation	Evening affirmations
Monday			
Tuesday			
Wednesday			
Thursday			
Friday			
Saturday			
Sunday			

Week 2
My affirmations

▸ I have a good job.

▸ ....

▸ ....

▸ ....

▸ ....

▸ ....

My visualisation

▸ Enjoying your inner child visualisation (see pages 115–6).

My checklist

Day	Morning affirmations	Visualisation	Evening affirmations
Monday			
Tuesday			
Wednesday			
Thursday			
Friday			
Saturday			
Sunday			

Week 3
My affirmations

▶ I am confident in my abilities.

▶ . . . .

▶ . . . .

▶ . . . .

▶ . . . .

▶ . . . .

My visualisation

▶ Getting back to work visualisation (see pages 117–8).

My checklist

Day	Morning affirmations	Visualisation	Evening affirmations
Monday			
Tuesday			
Wednesday			
Thursday			
Friday			
Saturday			
Sunday			

Week 4
My affirmations

▶ I radiate powerful positive energy.

▶ . . . .

▶ . . . .

▶ . . . .

▶ . . . .

▶ . . . .

My visualisation

▶ . . . .

My checklist

Day	Morning affirmations	Visualisation	Evening affirmations
Monday			
Tuesday			
Wednesday			
Thursday			
Friday			
Saturday			
Sunday			

Week 5
My affirmations

▸ I have a powerful presence.

▸ . . . . ▸ .

▸ . . . . ▸ .

▸ . . . . ▸ .

▸ . . . . ▸ .

▸ . . . . ▸ .

My visualisation

▸ . . . .

My checklist

Day	Morning affirmations	Visualisation	Evening affirmations
Monday			
Tuesday			
Wednesday			
Thursday			
Friday			
Saturday			
Sunday			

Week 6
My affirmations

▸   I am in control of my life.

▸   ....

▸   ....

▸   ....

▸   ....

▸   ....

My visualisation

▸   ....

My checklist

Day	Morning affirmations	Visualisation	Evening affirmations
Monday			
Tuesday			
Wednesday			
Thursday			
Friday			
Saturday			
Sunday			

Index